God's Currency

Sheila Holm

God's Currency

ISBN-13: 978-1497559721

ISBN-10: 1497559723

Unless otherwise indicated all scriptures are taken from the New King James version of the Bible.

HISBest4us@aol.com

Printed in USA by HIS Best Publishing

Dedication, In Grateful Acknowledgment

To the memory of my Father (1918-2011) who did not lose faith in the midst of crisis and always taught us to do the right thing and my Mother who has taught by example, Irvin and Clarice, and to my California family, my cousins LaVonne and Gene McGee, and to our ancestors who emigrated to America for religious freedom and stood firm in faith.

To Bishop George Dallas McKinney for the depth of prophetic understanding required, for being steadfast in helping me to keep on keepin' on, personally, encouraging me prior to and after each new adventure with God, while I remain grateful for your stand for all God sends to you!

To the memory (1918-2006) of Pastor Harald Bredesen, the friendship developed during meetings with and introductions arranged by him, especially for setting up my interview with Benny Hinn. For sharing front row studio seats because God orchestrated my attendance as a witness of the prophetic word from Benny Hinn that God would send a Muslim man with a salvation testimony and his name would be Nasir (Dr. Nasir Siddiki).

To Pastor Steve Dittmar, Jubilee Church, and to my host families during my visits, especially to Michael and Wendy Blomquist and to the powerful testimony of Christina Thee to confirm the faith level of children at four years old, and to her family for providing the Tommy Tenney books, plus to the many prayer partners and the multiple blessings received by participating at Jubilee after each assignment 'in a new way' as orchestrated by God.

To Pastor Earl Harrigan for being an amazing, anointed singer, especially ***Walk on the Water*** and ***All Rise,*** plus being a key witness to these days.

To John Willison for his mighty testimony and his offer to provide a tour of the TBN studio in Irving, Texas, a tour which has not happened, yet, however, it led to an introduction with the TBN producer, the opportunity to be interviewed on ***Praise The Lord,*** and for being the pilot who provided travel to a women's conference in Arkansas and to the Oklahoma church to encourage a pastor who was also from Nebraska. By the way, I'm still waiting for the promised tour of TBN.

To Big John Hall for confirming God introduced us at a Rodney Howard Browne meeting without sharing a word; God's plan when we were in each others' 'hometown.'

To Ken Blanchard, for understanding exactly where my life was and what was required to get me out from under the rock to stand firm on the rock once again while living beyond the 'world plans' by diving 100% into Kingdom business!

To Rodney Howard Browne for returning many times to San Diego at the exact time to renew the anointing that restores and prepares me to say YES for the next assignment.

To TD Jakes, Pastor Sam Ankrah and Pastor Charles Benneh and staff, to Bishop Duncan Williams and his worship team, to pastors & Bishops in London, especially Bishop John Francis for sharing the gift of his ***Finally*** CD, for the amazing contributions made during my journey.

To Pastor Mark Smallcomb for understanding the depth of ***God's Storehouse Principle*** message, yielding to God's structure, inviting me to share the details with business leaders and surrounding churches, including me within the Ed Silvoso meetings and for proclaiming the testimony of what God did when we came together on national TV (Australian version of CBS 60 Minutes).

To Pastor Rex Morgan for yielding to God so the Aboriginal Community could hear the message of ***God's Storehouse Principle*** and support the implementation during the service.

To Pastor Arnold in London for being so deeply touched by the message within ***God's Storehouse Principle*** that you were seeking the best of the best audio options to give me a copy so it would re-encourage me in the exact moment when I needed re-encouragement.

To Pastor Isileli for capturing ***God's Storehouse Principle*** before gathering the church together for fasting and prayer and remaining diligent until God confirmed it was time for us to meet together for God would change a nation if we stood firm together with our Lord.

To Prophet and Apostle John Kelly for prophetic words over my life and for referring me to Pastor Harold Dewberry.

To Bill in Tennessee for his depth and impeccable timing!

To Pastor Harold Dewberry for standing firm, delivering and releasing so many from what binds their heart and mind and returns them to a real relationship with Christ, for fasting and praying until God shared a clear message about me traveling down under and remaining in the country long enough for God to orchestrate the time and opportunity for me to meet with the Pastor in Fiji, a trip which unfolded weeks after you left your laptop with me and returned to America.

To the many pastors, evangelists, teachers, and fellow prophets and apostles, and the leadership of the church, the speakers and saints participating in the various seminars and conferences around the world who have invited me, encouraged me, prayed with me and introduced me to host families who have become part of my breath of life gift from God. To the prayer partners, intercessors and prayer warriors walking the wall, and to the memory of Jan Franklin (leaving us too soon on December 7, 2008), a powerful woman of God who joined me as a witness for California meetings and she became a valued prayer assistant with the long prayer lines, to Gary & Cindy Graham and to the memory (1953-2011) of 'Rozi' Graham Blegen, because in our lives God orchestrates the details as we gather together for in life ***It's A Faith Walk!*** with the Holy Spirit confirming our personal part within ***God's Storehouse Principle*** so the life we live within the Body of Christ will help all of us learn how to be set apart and operate within ***God's Currency.***

TABLE OF CONTENTS

Freedom Monument: Wikipedia. National Monument to the Forefathers; Please view the DVD *Monumental* for further details: www.monumentalmovie.com. Kirk Cameron embarks upon the Pilgrim's journey from England to America. It will deepen your faith. Friends are buying DVD copies of *Monumental* for their family and friends.

Martin Luther

"The whole being of any Christian is faith and love. Faith brings the person to God, love brings the person to people."

"Faith is a living and unshakable confidence, a belief in the grace of God so assured that a man would die a thousand deaths for its sake."

"I believe that I cannot by my own reason or strength believe in Jesus Christ, my Lord, or come to Him; but the Holy Ghost has called me by the Gospel, enlightened me with His gifts, sanctified and kept me in the true faith..."

Henrietta Mears

"Faith is caught rather than taught."

Robert Louis Stevenson

"Don't judge each day by the harvest you reap, but by the seeds you plant."

Foreword

In 'God's Currency' Sheila Holm affirms that the currency in the Kingdom of God is <u>Faith.</u>

The word of God clearly proclaims that the just shall live by faith and all things are possible to him that believeth. Time and time again Sheila has experienced the power of *God's Currency* when earthly resources were not available and she chose to spend *God's Currency* to fulfilling the work of the ministry.

She has discovered that *God's Currency* is honored because He honors faith that honors God.

By acknowledging the kingdom currency she encourages the believer to live a fully surrendered life to God and engage in a faith walk that honors God in every situation.

In this book the reader will be encouraged to honor God and follow his commandments, to be guided by the Holy Spirit, to teach others and make disciples; to live as God has instructed us.

In order to experience the gift of grace and have access to *God's Currency* we are encouraged to tithe, sow, harvest, store up and share the knowledge of prosperity with our fellow travelers so that we may bring increase to the Body of Christ.

It is an urgent message for us in these days as Sheila has boldly declared that if we were living our life based on *God's Currency* we would no longer be dependent upon the world system.

Bishop George Dallas McKinney

President, Pentecostal & Charismatic Churches North America (70,000+)

Board Member of Global Ministries: Billy Graham, Morris Cerullo, etc.

General Board Member, Church of God in Christ (COGIC)

Bishop and Pastor, St. Stephens Cathedral (COGIC)

Prologue

As Paul Established The Foundation of Fellowship

We are To Establish As The Church & Fellowship

And, Since We Are Each 'The Church'

We Are Responsible to Share God's Truth!

I've been asked so often if I am an Evangelist. God does evangelize through me, however, my heart is for those who came to Christ but, they were hurt / judged / ostracized by the 'well meaning Christians' within the fellowship.

As Paul traveled town to town, establishing 'the church' by discipling the people, equipping and training them with the truth and communicating with them regarding what is right and what is not quite right, the fellowship grew in each region. Due to how I express what God does through me and since I confirm I represent the God, the true I Am, I've had the opportunity to open the eyes and ears of so many pastors for they knew they were called but, they were disheartened due to the administrative structure of the denominational church.

The best way I can help us 'get on the same page' and gain the truth about the true structure is to direct you to Paul's letter to the people in Corinth.

Before you begin to take in the first four chapters of I Corinthians, please feel free to take a quick break. Get a cup of coffee, tea, water and a pen and paper or a journal to make notes as you view how we are to 'be' as 'the people of God, ambassadors of Christ, the church'.

This is a lot to take in.

The world influences are present and they can cause confusion, distractions, and sometimes it becomes like a radio station or movie playing in your mind while trying to read.

It helps to keep praise music playing everywhere in your home and office. You are seeking the deep things of God and the deeper you go the harder the enemy will work to confuse and distract you!

I had to read it a few times when God first directed me to His truth within the letter Paul sent to the Corinthians.

Personally, since this is a lot to digest I did not insert the next chapter(s). These four are the basics for us to comprehend as we work together to become sharpened, as iron sharpens iron!

You can read further while the intensity of the message increases. Can you imagine if Paul was writing to the current generation regarding what he heard about the activities within the homes, schools and businesses?

Often when I am asked to encourage a pastor, the higher levels within the denomination are not realizing the problems within the individual churches due to being 'out of alignment' themselves.

Are you ready to see what it would be like?

May I be one of the people you can count on who will absolutely encourage you when it seems too tough to carry on, to help you take a look at how we are operating 'in our relationship' with the e LORD. The closer we are to Him, the more Peculiar we become as People, His Peculiar People, His Holy Nation.

Are we able to become a people who are interested in uniting together as believers, being filled with Faith and guided by the Holy Spirit to go forward with the LORD on the journey, aka Faith Walk, He has laid out before us? Are we willing to be a people who will function together within His Storehouse Principle? Are we so we committed to becoming His Peculiar People, His Holy Nation, who are a people separate and set apart from the world, ready and able to operate within His Currency?

Once you are ready, I'll meet you at I Corinthians 1!

Paul's Letter To The People In Corinth

I Corinthians 1

Greeting:

Paul, called *to be* an apostle of Jesus Christ through the will of God, and Sosthenes *our* brother,

[2] ***To the church of God*** *which is at Corinth, to* ***those who are sanctified in Christ Jesus****, called to be saints,* ***with all who in every place call on the name of Jesus Christ our Lord, both theirs and ours:***

[3] ***Grace to you and peace from God our Father and the Lord Jesus Christ.***

Spiritual Gifts at Corinth:

[4] *I thank my God always concerning you* ***for the grace of God which was given to you by Christ Jesus****,* [5] ***that you were enriched in everything by Him in all utterance and all knowledge****,* [6] *even* ***as the testimony of Christ was confirmed in you****,* [7] ***so that you come short in no gift****, eagerly waiting for the revelation of our Lord Jesus Christ,* [8] *who will also confirm you to the end,* ***that you may be blameless in the day of our Lord Jesus Christ****.* [9] ***God is faithful, by whom you were called into the fellowship of His Son, Jesus Christ our Lord.***

Sectarianism Is Sin:

[10] *Now I plead with you, brethren, by the name of our Lord Jesus Christ,* ***that you all speak the same thing****, and* ***that there be no divisions among you****, but* ***that you be perfectly joined together in the same mind and in the same judgment****.* [11] *For it has been declared to me concerning you, my brethren, by those of Chloe's*

household, that there are contentions among you. [12] *Now I say this, that each of you says, "**I am of Paul,**" or "**I am of Apollos,**" or "**I am of Cephas,**" or "**I am of Christ.**"* [13] *Is Christ divided? Was Paul crucified for you? Or were you baptized in the name of Paul?*

[14] *I thank God that I baptized none of you except Crispus and Gaius,* [15] *lest anyone should say that I had baptized in my own name.* [16] *Yes, I also baptized the household of Stephanas. Besides, I do not know whether I baptized any other.* [17] *For **Christ did not send me to baptize, but to preach the gospel, not with wisdom of words, lest the cross of Christ should be made of no effect.***

Christ the Power and Wisdom of God:

[18] *For the message of the cross is foolishness to those who are perishing, but to us who are being saved it is the power of God.* [19] For it is written: "***I will destroy the wisdom of the wise, and bring to nothing the understanding of the prudent.***"

[20] *Where is the wise? Where is the scribe? Where is the disputer of this age? Has not God made foolish the wisdom of this world?* [21] *For since, in the wisdom of God, the world through wisdom did not know God, it pleased God through the foolishness of the message preached to save those who believe.* [22] *For Jews request a sign, and Greeks seek after wisdom;* [23] *but we preach Christ crucified, to the Jews a stumbling block and to the Greeks*

foolishness, [24] *but to those who are called, both Jews and Greeks, Christ the power of God and the wisdom of God.* [25] *Because* ***the foolishness of God is wiser than men,*** *and* ***the weakness of God is stronger than men.***

Glory Only in the Lord:

[26] *For you see your calling, brethren, that not many wise according to the flesh, not many mighty, not many noble,* ***are called.*** [27] *But God has chosen the foolish things of the world to put to shame the wise, and God has chosen the weak things of the world to put to shame the things which are mighty;* [28] *and the base things of the world and the things which are despised God has chosen, and the things which are not, to bring to nothing the things that are,* [29] *that no flesh should glory in His presence.* [30] *But of Him you are in Christ Jesus, who became for us wisdom from God —and righteousness and sanctification and redemption—* [31] that, as it is written, "***He who glories, let him glory in the Lord.***"

I Corinthians 2

And I, brethren, when I came to you, did not come with excellence of speech or of wisdom declaring to you the testimony of God. [2] *For I determined not to know anything among you except*

Jesus Christ and Him crucified. [3] *I was with you in weakness, in fear, and in much trembling.* [4] *And my speech and my preaching were not with persuasive words of human wisdom, but in demonstration of the Spirit and of power,* [5] *that your faith should not be in the wisdom of men but in the power of God.*

Spiritual Wisdom:

[6] *However, we speak wisdom among those who are mature, yet not the wisdom of this age, nor of the rulers of this age, who are coming to nothing.* [7] *But we speak the wisdom of God in a mystery, the hidden wisdom which God ordained before the ages for our glory,* [8] *which none of the rulers of this age knew; for had they known, they would not have crucified the Lord of glory.*

[9] But as it is written:

"***Eye has not seen,***

nor ear heard,

nor have entered into the heart of man

the things which God has ('in store')

prepared for those who love Him."

[10] *But* ***God has revealed them to us through His Spirit. For the Spirit searches all things, yes, the deep things of God.*** [11] *For what man knows the things of a man except the spirit of the man which is in him? Even so* ***no one knows the things of God except***

the Spirit of God. *[12] Now we have received, not the spirit of the world, but* ***<u>the Spirit who is from God, that we might know the things that have been freely given to us by God.</u>***

[13] These things we also speak, ***not in words which man's wisdom teaches but which the Holy Spirit teaches, comparing spiritual things with spiritual***. *[14] But the natural man does not receive the things of the Spirit of God, for they are foolishness to him; nor can he know* **them**, *because they are spiritually discerned. [15] But he who is spiritual judges all things, yet he himself is* **rightly** *judged by no one. [16] For "****who has known the mind of the Lord that he may instruct Him?"*** *But we have the mind of Christ.*

I Corinthians 3

Sectarianism Is Carnal:

And I, brethren, ***could not speak to you as to spiritual people but as to carnal, as to babes in Christ***. *[2]* ***I fed you with milk and not with solid food; for until now you were not able to receive it, and even now you are still not able***; *[3] for you are still carnal. For* ***where there are envy, strife, and divisions among you, are you not carnal and behaving like mere men? [4] For when one says, "I am of Paul," and another, "I am of Apollos," are you not carnal?***

Watering, Working, Warning:

[5] *Who then is Paul, and who is Apollos, but ministers through whom you believed, as the Lord gave to each one?* [6] ***I planted, Apollos watered, but God gave the increase.*** [7] *So then neither he who plants is anything, nor he who waters, but God who gives the increase.* [8] *Now* ***he who plants and he who waters are one, and each one will receive his own reward according to his own labor.***

[9] *For* ***<u>we are God's fellow workers</u>***; ***<u>you are God's field, you are God's building</u>***. [10] *According to the grace of God which was given to me,* ***<u>as a wise master builder I have laid the foundation, and another builds on it. But let each one take heed how he builds on it</u>***. [11] *For no other foundation can anyone lay than that which is laid, which is Jesus Christ.* [12] *Now if anyone builds on this foundation with gold, silver, precious stones, wood, hay, straw,* [13] *each one's work will become clear; for the Day will declare it, because it will be revealed by fire; and* ***<u>the fire will test each one's work, of what sort it is.</u>*** [14] *If anyone's work which he has built on it endures, he will receive a reward.* [15] *If anyone's work is burned, he will suffer loss; but he himself will be saved, yet so as through fire.*

[16] ***Do you not know that you are the temple of God and that the Spirit of God dwells in you?*** [17] ***If anyone defiles the temple of God, God will destroy him. For the temple of God is holy, which temple you are.***

Avoid Worldly Wisdom:

[18] *Let no one deceive himself. If anyone among you seems to be wise in this age, let him become a fool that he may become wise.* [19] ***For the wisdom of this world is foolishness with God.*** *For it is written,* ***"He catches the wise in their own craftiness"****;* [20] *and again,* ***"The Lord knows the thoughts of the wise, that they are futile."*** [21] *Therefore let no one boast in men. For all things are yours:* [22] *whether Paul or Apollos or Cephas, or the world or life or death, or things present or things to come—all are yours.* [23] *And* ***you are Christ's, and Christ is God's.***

I Corinthians 4

Stewards of the Mysteries of God:

Let a man so consider us, as servants of Christ and stewards of the mysteries of God. [2] *Moreover* ***it is required in stewards that one be found faithful.*** [3] *But with me it is a very small thing that I should be judged by you or by a human court. In fact, I do not even judge myself.* [4] *For I know of nothing against myself, yet I am not justified by this; but He who judges me is the Lord.* [5] *Therefore judge nothing before the time, until the Lord comes, who will both bring to light the hidden things of darkness and reveal the counsels of the hearts. Then each one's praise will come from God.*

Fools for Christ's Sake:

[6] *Now these things, brethren, I have figuratively transferred to myself and Apollos for your sakes,* ***that you may learn in us not to think beyond what is written, that none of you may be puffed up on behalf of one against the other.*** [7] *For who makes you differ from another? And what do you have that you did not receive? Now if you did indeed receive it, why do you boast as if you had not received it?*

[8] ***You are already full! You are already rich! You have reigned as kings without us—and indeed I could wish you did reign, that we also might reign with you!*** [9] *For I think that God has displayed us, the apostles, last, as men condemned to death; for we have been made a spectacle to the world, both to angels and to men.* [10] ***We are fools for Christ's sake, but you are wise in Christ! We are weak, but you are strong! You are distinguished, but we are dishonored!*** [11] ***To the present hour we both hunger and thirst, and we are poorly clothed, and beaten, and homeless.*** [12] ***And we labor, working with our own hands. Being reviled, we bless; being persecuted, we endure;*** [13] ***being defamed, we entreat. We have been made as the filth of the world, the offscouring of all things until now.***

Paul's Paternal Care:

[14] ***I do not write these things to shame you, but as my beloved children I warn you.*** [15] *For though you might have ten thousand instructors in Christ, yet you do not have many fathers; for in Christ Jesus I have begotten you through the gospel.* [16] ***Therefore I urge you, imitate me.*** [17] ***For this reason I have sent Timothy to you, who is my beloved and faithful son in the Lord, who will remind you of my ways in Christ, as I teach everywhere in every church.***

[18] ***Now some are puffed up, as though I were not coming to you.*** [19] *But I will come to you shortly,* ***if the Lord wills****, and* ***I will know, not the word of those who are puffed up, but the power.*** [20] *For* ***the kingdom of God is not in word but in power.*** [21] ***What do you want? Shall I come to you with a rod, or in love and a spirit of gentleness?***

This is a lot to take in.

May I be one of the people you can count on who will absolutely re-encourage you when it seems too tough to carry on, to help you take a look at how we are operating 'in our relationship' with the LORD. Remember, the closer we are to Him, the more Peculiar we become as People, His Peculiar People, His Holy Nation.

Knowing what we are to do and how we are to proceed: Are we able to become a people who are interested in uniting together as believers, being filled with Faith and guided by the Holy Spirit to go forward with the LORD on the journey, aka Faith Walk, He has laid out before us? Are we willing to be a people who will function together within His Storehouse Principle? Are we so we committed to becoming His Peculiar People, His Holy Nation, who are a people separate and set apart from the world, ready and able to operate within His Currency?

Lord help us hear and see Your truth clearly!

Help us learn how to disciple each other!

Help us see the needs of others as You see them!

Help us become equipped and trained in these days!

Help us listen to the truth and be sharpened by each other as iron sharpens iron!

Keep Your hand upon us!

You may want to spend some more time to make a few notes or review your notes.

This example may help bring us back to what is going on within us and within the world for the LORD is the same yesterday, today and tomorrow!

In **John 5:19+, John 8:28-29 and John 12:44-50,** our Jesus Christ, our LORD & Savior, our joint heir due to making each of us sons of the Father, made it clear! I only do what I see the Father do and I only say what I hear the Father say!

I've just heard about a young man named Daniel who was so frustrated in the seminary training he wanted to quit. He was so frustrated that he told God: ***I only want to go where You want me to go and do what You want me to do.***

He read the scripture again and left the seminary that day.

The LORD told Daniel what the next step would be: ***Go to Yemen and take a new bible with you to give away.***

Daniel was immediately concerned and expressed his concern to our Father: ***Lord, Yemen is a Muslim country!***

Amazing when we try to tell the LORD what we think the LORD does not know. Trusting it also makes us look quite funny to Him! Grateful He has a sense of humor!

The LORD was clear and specific by repeating Daniel's desire: ***Do you want to go where I want you to go and do what I want you to do?***

Daniel was humbled and said, ***Yes LORD.***

He purchased a new bible and flew to Yemen.

During his prayer time in the hotel, he asked the LORD what he was supposed to do with the bible. The LORD said, ***Tomorrow you will go to (address) and give the bible to the family in that home.*** Daniel was nervous as the address was in the Muslim section.

The LORD knew his concern and asked him again, ***Do you want to go where I want you to go and do what I want you to do?***

Again Daniel was humbled. He responded, ***Yes LORD.***

The next morning the man went to the exact address provided by the LORD with the bible 'in hand' when he knocked on the door.

The father of the family answered the door. When he opened the door it revealed all in the home were in Muslim attire.

Daniel handed the bible to the man who immediately rejoiced. He was in tears. The family rejoiced with him.

The man was in tears as he asked for Daniel's name. When Daniel revealed his name, the family members cried, thanked the LORD and hugged Daniel.

Daniel was in shock.

The father explained: ***Last night Jesus came to our home. He told us that He was sending His representative Daniel to our home today with a bible so we could read and know the truth.***

Are we willing to go where the LORD needs us to go, do what He needs us to do and say only what He wants us to say?

Take all the time you need.

When you are ready, I'll meet you at Chapter 1.

Smith Wigglesworth

"Great faith is the product of great fights. Great testimonies are the outcome of great tests. Great triumphs can only come out of great trials."

Kenneth Copeland

"God's plan for your life is bigger than everything coming against it."

Andrew Murray

"Every exhibition of the power of faith was the fruit of a special revelation from God ... Our spiritual power depends on God Himself speaking those promises to us."

Aimee Semple McPherson

"You don't need to be an orator. What God wants is plain people with the good news in their hearts, who are willing to go and tell it to others. The love of winning souls for Jesus Christ sets a fire burning in one's bones. Soul-winning is the most important thing in the world. All I have is on the altar for the Lord and while I have my life and strength, I will put my whole being into the carrying out of this Great Commission."

Chapter 1 Individually, We Are The Church

If you missed the Prologue, please go back to page 11. I promise you will be very glad you did!

If we were living our life based upon God's Currency, as though we truly are the Church, the Body of Christ, it would not matter if the national or world-based currency crashed because it would not affect us.

Psalm 24:1

The earth *is* the LORD's, and all its fullness,

the world and those who dwell therein.

I Corinthians 10:26

for *"the earth is the Lord's, and all its fullness."*

I realize it may seem like a far stretch today because there has been so much focus upon money, either the world currency or a national currency. However, over time this is what has become our focus because we have compromised with the world so much we have become dependent upon the world structure:

Money makes the world go round!

When I finished ***God's Storehouse Principle*** book and workbook within a few weeks of ***It's A Faith Walk!*** Being released, I was sure it was time for a rest or a new assignment.

It was a shock to hear God talk about a third book.

When God confirmed ***God's Currency***, I reminded God that I mentioned it within ***God's Storehouse Principle.***

Since the faith and storehouse messages are strong messages for the Body of Christ today, I felt people needed a bit more time to digest it, also.

However, God quickly reminded me of the message He shared through me when I was interviewed for a cable TV broadcast.

The interviewer wanted to know what God was focused upon right now. It did not show in my face when the program aired however, I was in a very quick and intense conversation with God. Without taking my next breath, I already heard my voice saying, ***God's Currency.***

Then the host asked me why. Again, the LORD provided the response without any indication of changes in my facial expression while it was clearly my voice which stated, ***The body of Christ needs to be equipped and trained to live by faith, function within God's Storehouse to become a separate and set apart people operating within God's Currency so when the currency or rules changes within a nation or the world, the body of Christ would not be affected.***

Wow. That made a lot of sense.

The host provided a DVD copy of the interview. I quickly fast forwarded to the part where she asked the question and tears flowed. I had to ask God, ***Is it possible?*** He reminded me that I asked for the flow amongst the believers in America and in Europe as the people expressed within Africa. The LORD confirmed these steps are key to the equipping and training, the discipleship of the believers so we walk together in faith, share from the storehouse and sharpen each other as iron sharpens iron so we will operate together with Him within His currency as a people separate and set apart from the world.

Immediately, the message which touched me so deeply the tears flowed resulted in a quick phone call to Bishop McKinney. Love the LORD however, I have to admit that I was hopeful Bishop would say it was too soon to release another book. However, instead of asking about my concerns or thoughts, Bishop merely asked what the LORD said the book would be about.

While I was sharing the specifics with Bishop he kept saying, ***Yes. That's right. Good. When can you have the outline to me?***

Yikes. I've never liked outlines.

My first thought was outline option is a good delay option.

However, before I could respond Bishop said, ***I'll be on a flight in the morning and not returning for seven days. So, send your outline to me in seven days.***

A deadline. I've never liked deadlines, either.

There is a lot of surrendering required to be obedient to what our LORD asks of us! Layers and layers of surrendering. Each time resistance comes up, I realize there is more for me to learn about surrendering!

I thanked Bishop and told him I would submit everything to him in seven days.

Then, I went to God because He clearly knew I did not like outlines or deadlines. I needed His help now.

The LORD merely requested, ***Sit with me.***

I can tell you now what I could not tell you then. The LORD helped with all details and the manuscript was ready to share with Bishop in seven days. There was a bit more panic or resistance with intensity at times when the LORD wanted a prologue, etc., since an entire chapter moved up to the front of the book before Chapter 1. However, He has clearly proved His ways are not our ways and due to not liking outlines or deadlines, the LORD worked side-by-side with me to complete the draft copy within seven days.

Bishop called to say he would review the outline but, he wanted to know why it was so long. When I explained how he received a lot more than an outline, he laughed and said he would provide the Foreword for the book. Within minutes, Bishop's assistant sent the Foreword by email.

Again, tears flowed as this experience is another seven day example of the flow our LORD provides when we are operating within His currency. He reminds us what He is in our life each time since what we do with and for Him on earth so it will become on earth as it is in heaven is about a lot more than money. ***God's Currency*** is actually how we are to operate in our life with Him while on earth and as joint heirs with Christ our life is clearly about a whole lot more than money!

It is God's plan for us to become His people, a peculiar people, a holy nation, living with Him, separate and set apart from the world.

There is absolutely an urgency in God's promptings due in large part to the fact the distinctions between the believers and the non-believers is not easily evident in most settings 'in the world' outside of the time spent within a service or meeting at a church or a bible study. LORD help us!

Lord help us to become a people who do not depend upon or live according to the world-based plan!

Lord help us right the wrongs for the world plans are affecting multiple generations.

Lord thank you for drawing us close to You. Renewing and restoring our hearts with your truth each day when we commune with You.

Lord help us become Your ambassadors. Help us learn how to express Your love for people each time we are with the people. Thank You for keeping Your hand upon us in our Faith Walk while we learn how to function according to Your Storehouse Principle so we will become a separate and set apart people operating within Your Currency.

Help us navigate through the process for Your sake and for the sake of our lives, our families, our extended families, our nation and the world.

Lord we thank You for 2nd chances, for Your grace and mercy. And most of all Lord we thank you for loving us in spite of us!!! AMEN.

I prayed for a good example of how much our Lord loves us and how much He is misunderstood by us because we do not readily recognize His gifts, blessings and currency.

This email has cycled through a few times and it has meant a lot to me each time I read it as a reminder of our Father's love. In the moment I cried out for the example my friend Bill in Tennessee sent me the email this time. I have received it before and it means as much each time. Thank you Father! This message is the direct answer to my prayer:

FATHER, I WANTED A CAR NOT A BIBLE

A young man was getting ready to graduate from college. For many months he had admired a beautiful sports car in a dealer's showroom and knowing his father could well afford it, he told him that was all he wanted.

As Graduation Day approached, the young man awaited signs that his father had purchased the car. Finally, on the morning of his graduation his father called him into his private study. He told him how proud he was to have such a fine son and how much he loved him. He handed him a beautifully wrapped gift box.

Curious but. somewhat disappointed the young man opened the box and found a lovely, leather-bound Bible with his name embossed in gold. Angrily, he raised his voice to his father and said,***" With all your money you give me a Bible?"***

He stormed out of the house, leaving the Bible behind.

Many years passed and the young man was very successful in business. He had a beautiful home and a wonderful family when he realized his father was getting on in years. He thought perhaps he should go to see him because he had not seen him since that graduation day.

But, before he could make arrangements he received a telegram confirming his father had passed away and the will left all of his father's worldly possessions to him.

Now, he needed to go home immediately and take care of things.

When he arrived at his father's house, sadness and regret filled his heart. He began to search through his father's office for important documents. He saw the Bible he was given by his father on his graduation day. It still looked new, just as he had left it years ago.

With tears, he opened the Bible and began to turn the pages. His father had carefully underlined a verse, **Matthew 7:11.** ***"If you then, being evil, know how to give good gifts to your children, how much more will your Father who is in heaven give good things to those who ask Him!"***

As he read those words, a car key dropped from the back of the Bible. It had a tag with the dealer's name, the same dealer who had the sports car he had desired during his final year in college. On the tag he noticed the exact date of his graduation with the words...**PAID IN FULL.**

As believers in Christ, our bill is PAID IN FULL!

Do we merely toss it aside, get angry because we want more, either something else or something different than God arranged? How many times do we miss God's blessings because we are focused only upon exactly what we want and how we want it? Since we do not know God's plans in advance or what He is preparing for us since the scriptures are true:

I Corinthians 2:9. But as it is written: "***Eye has not seen, nor ear heard, nor have entered into the heart of man the things which God has ('in store') prepared for those who love Him.***"

What if we operated as though we knew our LORD never leaves us or forsakes us? For the truth is we have no idea what God sees or what God is up to on our behalf for our LORD's ways are not our ways. So, who are we as believers when our LORD sends blessings which are not packaged as we expected?

In ***God's Storehouse Principle*** I share a story about a man's vision during his surgery. The LORD walked him through heaven and showed him the ***Storehouse.*** Inside, the man was shown many shelves with the unopened boxes of blessings wrapped in glossy white paper and red bows. Blessings awaiting delivery.

God's Plan

I am one person and I am as surprised as you are that God would prompt me to proceed with the release of the three books in such quick succession.

However, there is an urgency because the Body of Christ is split into separate sections while the world is in deep trouble.

We are each the church.

We can affect a change, if we will stand firm to do it!

We are to seek where and when we can bless, daily!

We are to encourage each other in the faith, daily!

We are to help each other to remain filled with faith!

We are to listen to the Father, do what He does and say what He says as Jesus confirmed!

We are the reason why the flow of *God's Currency* stopped!

Lord we thank you for keeping your hand upon us and speaking to us in our waking and resting hours so we will become filled with faith, functioning within your storehouse principle as a separate and set apart people operating in your currency so the lost will see who You are in us and hunger for You and come to You to learn Your truth!

Many have given up on God due to their need not being met as they expected. Hard to blame them when they do not know what is possible. We are not being discipled, not supported with bible-based and spirit-filled instructions while seeking to be fully equipped and trained for these days.

The Body of Christ is in trouble. **This status was NOT God's plan for us!**

If we were individually operating 'as the Church' and fully functioning together as the Body of Christ we would be walking forward and speaking our faith, sharing storehouse resources with each other and those our LORD directs us to bless. We would know who we could talk to or trust within a position of authority in the body of Christ and in the business world for we would discern the truth, seeks God's truth about them, and the LORD would know how to connect us with someone who knows them within our eternal networking structure.

Few people are fully aligned with God's truth and even fewer are proceeding per the guidance of the Holy Spirit. Without having the right structure in place, we are left on our own 'in the world' to figure out how to proceed.

Going Numb

aka Politically Correct Being So Important

About Things of No Importance

The Lord provided a specific plan.

His word is true.

God is the same yesterday, today and tomorrow.

God founded 'the church' upon the apostles & prophets, with Christ as the Chief Cornerstone. And, he made some to be evangelists, pastors and teachers. He gave us a firm foundation.

Over time, we narrowed down to making pastors responsible and accountable for everything. Find the people, evangelize until they come to the church building and contribute from their earnings. Then, be their pastor and teach them each week, plus be their prophet and their apostle as needed. Not easy and not right!

What we need for each of us to proceed as the church in our daily life was already provided. We are responsible and accountable to get beyond the word a week phase and become the body of Christ which the lost will know when we are in their midst!

Point the Compass to God

There is a lot that we never learned.

There is a structure for us to operate within.

No matter where we are in the world, focus upon God.

No matter what someone says about us, refer to God's word.

No matter what we think is right, ask the Holy Spirit.

God arranged life for us to live abundantly & prosper!

Feel Free to Do Everything I Do

Copy Me In All You See Me Do & Say

Christ Confirmed This Truth

This is the goal for us, individually as 'the Church' within the world, today.

Often I have stated, ***"It matters not that you remember my name. What does matter is that when you hear God's message through me you know God sent a woman your way and since that moment nothing about your life looks the same."***

A dear friend who heard me speak when I was in her area last month called to tell me that one of her closest friends was so deeply touched by what God shared through me that she said: ***"Her life is like the people in the Bible ... she lives with God like the people did in the Bible."***

This was God's plan for each of us.

A high compliment indeed! And, an answer to prayer.

I pray this becomes our experience, daily! Really!

As I have shared many times, people knew me as a wealthy woman with means. I had some significant world success. But, I would not trade any of those experiences or years for the moments with God and my life with Him today.

Now, I have been able to share many times with people per God's prompting: ***"Feel free to copy me in everything I do and say."*** It's discipleship with 100% willingness to be sharpened!

This is how God wants us to live, guided each day!

It did NOT happen for me over night!

I was NOT easy for God to deal with!

Instead of living as God planned, everything in life supported my participation in the world-based success plan. I learned it from many sources, education, friends and mentors.

Prior to the three years of travel with God, I was dealing with the world issues without discipleship. It was not pretty!

Plus, I was attending church every Sunday and tithing. But, I was not equipped and trained. I was not speaking about what God was doing in my life. I did not have that connection or understanding. I had lost it 'over time' due to the compromises with the world plan!

Everything I did was 'in line' I thought. But, I was not distinguishing a major difference between the success in the world and the prosperous life God provides and arranges for us.

People immediately gravitated to me and we had amazing conversations. However, they were not conversations which provided clarity about a life focused upon living as though it really mattered ... **life or death.**

This is the difference I briefly mentioned within ***God's Storehouse Principle.*** Typically we are taught to recognize the difference between right and wrong. What we are missing with the teaching is the closest counterfeit knows the same distinction and quotes scripture. Plus, often states the name of Jesus. **We need to know the difference between what is right and what is not quite right!**

Example: I was having a casual conversation with a woman and her young son during a return flight. She was very cordial and wanted to invite me to her annual church luncheon. Before we parted she said, ***"You will like the people. The Christian part at the beginning is for believers and they will be doing some bible study so you can skip the Christian part and just come for the luncheon. I will introduce you ..."***

It was a wake-up call. Social conversation during our entire journey together did not confirm for her that I was a Christian. She thought she was inviting a 'world-based' gal who did not know Christ as her Savior.

This happened to me during the time frame of owning my corporation (aka an all about me time frame, proceeding upon my plan for my retirement), and I was working diligently to please people of all faiths. Many of the clients were attorneys who were Jewish.

I specifically remember a Christmas when I issued three sets of cards:

1. Christian cards,
2. Holiday cards, without referring to Christ,
3. Beige and brown generic message sent to all of the people to be politically correct with people of all faiths

Easter was about the same:

1. Christian cards
2. Holiday cards
3. However, nothing for the people of other faiths

Lord keep your hand upon us! Help us know what to do when it is clear we know not what we are doing!

Chapter 2 In Fellowship Together, We Are The Church

Who Knew?

Not once did I hear that December 25 is not Christ's Birthday or that the day was merged with a pagan holiday. It has caused many to think Christianity is a false religion as the date is actually the date of the birth of the sons of the sun god. Check with a Google search and you will notice venom in the comments of the people who found out the truth and think the lies are the basis of the beliefs of the Body of Christ. **Lord help us do better!**

Personally, it was new news to me when a man spit at me and told me I am perpetuating the lies. So I've asked many people, missionaries and pastors, who have attended seminary and they already knew the factual history and how Constantine or his mother merged Christian details with pagan holidays and rituals, to have Jesus be a topic.

I wanted to see the truth in scripture! It's there. The scriptures confirm the truth about Christmas trees and decorations: **Jeremiah 10:3-5:** For the customs of the peoples *are* futile; For *one* **cuts a tree from the forest**, The work of the hands of the workman, with the ax. [4] They **decorate it with silver and gold**; They **fasten it with nails and hammers so that it will not topple**. [5] They *are* upright, like a palm tree, and they cannot speak; They must be carried, because they cannot go *by themselves.* Do not be afraid of them, for they cannot do evil, **nor can they do any good**."

Lord keep your hand upon us. Help us do a better job of discipleship, to equip and train current and future generations. Lord help us train the people, especially the youth in Your truth!

As soon as I learned this fact was the truth, I reeled in the celebration of pagan / world-based holiday rituals. I stopped buying and participating in putting items on a tree cut from the forest. **As a body of believers, we can save millions of trees! Lord help us align and make a huge difference!**

I pray with every word shared you will be encouraged to seek the truth in God's word and celebrate the Feast of Tabernacles with great joy for that is the time frame (fall) which is calculated as: birth of Christ & Epiphany due to timing defined within scriptures. Scholars have aligned the dates of Mary's visit with the mother of

John the Baptist & his birth. The truth is known but, the Body of Christ is unaware.

Not once did I hear Easter is also merged with a pagan holiday & pagan rituals are still being done by Christians due to lack of knowledge. If we knew the truth, we would not be competing to have the most colored eggs at our church! **We carried forward the pagan rituals of ancient times!Hosea 4:6:** ***My people are destroyed for lack of knowledge...***

Lord forgive us for we knew not what we were doing!

Nobody Discipled Me in this, but God!

Nobody Equipped and Trained Me about this, but God!

When God Provided Wisdom; Man confirmed 'we knew'!

Then, God Stepped In and Took My Hand

There was so much I needed to learn. I quickly realized the years of church attendance did not prepare me!

It took me a long time to find a bible-based and spirit-filled church.

I remember the first time I stepped into St. Stephen's Cathedral, Church of God in Christ, and I heard the praise team and choir sing.

It was a two dozen Kleenex experience as I soaked in the depth of God's love expressed by each voice. It took a few months before I reduced to about one dozen Kleenex.

The testimonies of the youth … what they have experienced … the battles they face but, God reaches them in the midst of their cries and provides a powerful answer … inspiring.

Then, Bishop McKinney speaks; all from God. No three point sermon with a bit of humor mixed in and no time limit!

Sometimes we are still in worship from the 8 AM service when the 11 AM service needs to begin. Praise God!

When we do potlucks, it's for both services and it typically benefits a program for the youth.

Then, I was blessed to be a witness of a mighty blessing.

Pastor Ray Bentley the founder (1979) of Maranatha Chapel in Rancho Bernardo expressed an amazing love for Bishop McKinney and St. Stephen's Cathedral when Maranatha's church family began their blessing with $25,000 cash. They obtained donations from businesses and hours and hours and hours of time (plumbers, tilers, painters, masons, electricians, carpet layers, caterers, and the list goes on & on) with donations obtained and hours volunteered from St. Stephen's members, also, resulting in a $250,000 **"Extreme Make-Over: Church Edition."**

Lord help us hear & see what we can do to bless & help us do all we can 'beyond money' to make it happen!

God Shifted My Focus To The People, The Church

God wants us to comprehend how to operate according to His plans and with His currency being shared one to another. There is a lot for us to do!

When God directed my attention to Jonah 4, I trusted I knew the Jonah story. However, Jonah 4 was a wake-up call.

God had provided for Jonah. The vine was there to give Jonah shelter at night but, Jonah became angry when it withered in the sunlight. Jonah was upset with God. God shifted Jonah's thinking, adjusted his view / focus. And, as God prompted me to read the book of Jonah, it shifted my thinking also for it is NOT about us for we did not make the vine or provide the vine as God did for Jonah in Chapter 4. Our life is NOT about us & asking for every need.

God is a big God, He has big plans for us and He sees the big picture. His heart is focused upon the people who will perish if we do not share the truth. God was pointing out to Jonah (to me, and now, to each of us) it's time to focus upon God's plan.

Jonah 4:10-11.

But the Lord said, "***You have had pity on the plant for which you have not labored, nor made it grow, which came up in a night and perished in a night.*** [11] ***And should I not pity Nineveh, that great city, in which are more than one hundred and twenty thousand persons who cannot discern between their right hand and their left—and much livestock?***"

As God's People We Are The Church, The Body of Christ

We may be 'it' for someone; the only person who speaks life into their life & breathes life into their situation. If we are not in tune with God's plan, we miss a once in a 'lifetime' opportunity. A life may be lost due to us not getting 'it' … God has sent people to me who want to commit suicide. I never thought I would have those thoughts since I thought only crazy people had those thoughts. But, situations 'in the world' are often crazy! Over time, I had a new mantra: ***Jesus take my hand and bring me home or bring me through!*** I was OK with either answer after reading Jonah 4 and realizing Jonah thought he had no reason to stay on earth.

Personally, I did not realize that the agents heard God's wisdom through me. There is no way 'on earth' or 'in the world' I would know the details God shared with me. God revealed what was going on 'behind the scenes' so the unjust within the justice system could be brought to justice.

Imagine what it must be like for the agents to hear this woman show up and give them information nobody would know unless they were in the room and in on the deal! I just wanted my life back. I tried even harder, because I did not deserve to bring them the truth and be destroyed after following their instructions. But, instead of clearing up any of the issues they erased me from the system and now the agents "have no current or prior file'. The world / enemy steals, kills and destroys.

The enemy lies!

But, regardless of the world plan: **We Are God's Temple, God's Treasure!**

We all experience issues.

How we face them and deal with them as God's people makes a huge difference!

The top agent asked me: ***"We just want to know, how did you come through all of this and not commit suicide?"*** The answer was easy, ***"God!"***

May our answer to the world always be as easy for the truth is the truth, our LORD provides all we need and want and as believers and joint heirs our bill is already PAID IN FULL.

Chapter 3 God's Currency vs. World Currency

A man was visited by Jesus one afternoon. Jesus told him the time was short because he would be going to heaven that night.

The man immediately began to make a plan. He pulled down a large suitcase before he realized he had no idea what the fashion would be like in heaven.

Then, he panicked a bit because he realized he had very little time to cash in all of his stocks, bonds and bank accounts. He immediately left his home and did just that.

When he returned home with the stacks of cash and he began to pack all of the bundles into the suitcase, he panicked again because he had no idea if heaven's currency would be the same as the currency of his country.

The man left his home again and rushed to meet with a currency exchange expert. The two men quickly agreed upon gold as the best currency since it is a currency recognized everywhere in the world.

The man realized the large suitcase would be quite heavy to carry when the bars of gold were inserted, so he decided to use two smaller suitcases. He put both suitcases on top of his bed so he could easily lay down between them in his best suit and tie, and still keep a good grip on both handles. He felt ready. He trusted he was fully prepared and ready to go to heaven at any time during the night.

He was at the pearly gates before he realized he had passed away. He was pleased to realize his hands were still in a tight grip, holding the handles of the suitcases so he was confident God would be pleased to see what he brought as soon as he entered heaven. However, God did not appear.

The man asked St. Peter when he would be able to meet with God. St. Peter reminded the man that God is very busy with the living. The man was visibly frustrated while he explained he brought something in the suitcases for God and he wanted to give it to Him in person. St. Peter smiled as he assured the man he would do everything he could to help.

St. Peter directed the man to a different building and recommended that he wait there and God would meet with him as soon as He could.

The man was excited. He entered the large building and God appeared within a moment.

The man was in awe of God's glory and rendered speechless when God asked, ***"What would you like to meet with me about?"*** Tears were evident even though he was beaming ear to ear when he handed the cases to God.

God opened the first case and said, ***"Gold bricks. Pavement. You brought me more pavement?"***

Perhaps this humor confirms the view many have seen when they have experienced spending a few moments in heaven and returned to say: ***The streets of heaven are paved with gold.*** And, I'm not picturing the yellow brick road in the ***Wizard of Oz*** only the real, gold bricks or bars which average 400 ounces. Gold on the market averages between $1200 and $1500/troy ounce.

God Created The Gold And The Gems

I have witnessed the gold and oil which are produced by God because of His blessing upon a woman who lost her organs to cancer. She was at death's door. She asked God if she could be saved long enough to see her daughter grow up and be married.

God gave her all new organs.

Now, each time she shares her testimony, pure gold flakes (they resemble snow flakes and no two are alike) so pure, it has been confirmed by gem analysts that the gold is real and it shocks them because it was not mined from the earth. She appears normal when she begins speaking. There is no evidence of the gold or oil. As soon as she completes the introductory portion of her talk and begins to share her testimony everything changes. The fragrant oil actually comes through her skin, even her scalp with the gold flakes falling and the oil dripping from her hair.

In fact, she has to stop frequently to gather the gold flakes and wipe the anointing oil so she can continue to see the people as she shares her testimony.

I have met people from churches experiencing the gold and gems being deposited within their church buildings. Some of the families are experiencing the perfect gems (proven to be real and formed but not cut by a machine or mined from the earth) and gold appearing in their homes.

The truth is: God created and provided all that is in and on the earth. Remember: **If we were living our life based upon God's Currency, as though we truly are the Church / the Body of Christ, it would not matter if the national or world-based currency crashed because we would not be affected.**

Psalm 24:1

The earth *is* the LORD's, and all its fullness,
the world and those who dwell therein.

I Corinthians 10:26

for *"the earth is the Lord's, and all its fullness."*

The world's currency structure is in a constant state of flux and more and more people are living in lack because they do not know the truth. God keeps it very simple.

We have made it complex.

How? We have isolated from each other vs. living as one body in one accord. Many have become dependent upon the world based plan and worldly government structure due to no guidance. We allowed it by compromising with the world.

We were to be set apart and disciple others in the truth.

Instead, due to compromising with the world so often over time and in so many areas of life, we do not know what God's plan is or the difference between living God's plan per God's word without allowing the world / enemy to influence our life and family, personally or as part of the Body of Christ.

God's Currency is what we are to be living by for it meets needs, fulfills dreams and plans and is the option to sustain us through any disaster we may face while 'in the world' during our lifetime. We have not lived according to God's **exchange** rate. His currency rate is all that matters!

The national or world currency, the money focus has affected every aspect of the church and our lives, so the church does not resemble God's structure in scripture. In **John 10:10,** *Jesus confirmed that He came so that we might have life, and have it more abundantly!*

In the past 2000 years what have we accomplished?

It would be great to hear God asking the famous Dr. Phil (an American TV host) question, especially if God used Dr. Phil's Texas, Southern accent: ***So, how's it (world plan) working for y'all?***

Since we are the church, the Body of Christ and we have been at this process for 2000 years what's your answer?

Lord forgive us. In many ways, we have forgotten who we are while we knew not what we did!

Paraphrasing scripture:

We are more than conquerors.

We are the head and not the tail.

Our Father owns the cattle on a thousand hills.

We are joint heirs with Christ.

Joint Heirs With Christ

Romans 8:16-18

The Spirit Himself bears witness with our spirit that we are children of God, [17] and if children, then heirs—heirs of God and joint heirs with Christ, if indeed we suffer with *Him,* that we may also be glorified together.

From Suffering to Glory [18] For I consider that the sufferings of this present time are not worthy *to be compared* with the glory which shall be revealed in us.

We are brothers and sisters as believers in Christ, making us saved sons and daughters of God. We are to know God's truth and disciple others to operate in life as Christ did with the guidance of the Holy Spirit. Christ confirmed even greater things would we be able to do, as the Church the Body of Christ. ***God's Currency*** at work!

Doing Our Father's Business, Kingdom Business While On Earth

We are to be about our Father's business, Kingdom business.

John 5:19-23

"Most assuredly, I say to you, the Son can do nothing of Himself, but what He sees the Father do; for whatever He does, the Son also does in like manner. [20] *For the Father loves the Son, and shows Him all things that He Himself does; and He will show Him greater works than these, that you may marvel.* [21] *For as the Father raises the dead and gives life to them, even so the Son gives life to whom He will.* [22] *For the Father judges no one, but has committed all judgment to the Son,* [23] *that all should honor the Son just as they honor the Father. He who does not honor the Son does not honor the Father who sent Him.*

John 14:12-14. The Answered Prayer

"Most assuredly, I say to you, he who believes in Me, the works that I do he will do also; and greater *works* than these he will do, because I go to My Father. [13] And whatever you ask in My name, that I will do, that the Father may be glorified in the Son. [14] If you ask anything in My name, I will do *it*.

Forgive Us Lord For Accepting The World Plan
Forgive Us For We Knew Not What We Did!

Most situations put people and families into crisis.

Example: Orphans are left in a government, foster care system. Even families in crisis are finding the government is able to 'lawfully remove their children and place them in the foster care system' until the courts decide where the children should live. Pastors are now 'bound by law' to turn in children and families after sharing issues with the pastor which new laws state are to be 'reviewed by the courts'.

We have not protected the children of the current and future generations or the widows. In churches throughout Europe the prior centuries they kept lists of the needs of the widows and families for the orphans. The provision of the need was documented whether the widow needed a piece of coal to keep warm in winter, grain to make bread or as an orphan the list stated families in the church 'making room'.

Often, there are discussions about the problems with the foster care system, issues with the 'homeless' and the 'aging' while it is up to us as the Body of Christ to stand firm with each other. In doing so, we would be a people living in the world and yet not of the world, set apart from the world vs. resembling the people of the world.

Homeless

I was invited to meet with a local church about the homeless issue in the community. The weather is consistently nice in Southern California, so many of the homeless from across America end up in the region.

The church was feeding the homeless moments before the meeting while people from various churches within the denomination were arriving.

Three of the homeless, a man and two teenagers (a boy and girl, both between 18 and 19 years old), wanted to attend the meeting.

The people were visibly opposed as the three had not showered in a few weeks or months. However, due to God's prompting, I asked the pastor to invite them and ask the man to open the meeting in prayer. As the man opened his bible, one of the people attending asked where he got the bible.

The man calmly stated he had learned the value of God's word in the midst of his crisis and even though many would grab photos when they are leaving their home due to a crisis, he knew he would not be able to carry photo albums with him while homeless. He knew the one thing he would need was his Bible. He said it has been a blessing because he knew he would be able to remember the people in the photos but he would want to be sure he had the true word with him on the streets when he needed it. The two teenagers found each other on the streets. They bonded in large part due to their stories being identical. Their mothers married again after the divorce. Their step-father's abused them and wanted them out of the house and on their own when they turned 18.

Widows

St. Stephen's built one tower across the street, keeping all ages together within the Body. It was so successful, a second tower was added. Jobs and Christian Fellowship & Blessings flow. A better option than government housing for seniors! What else can be done? What is God saying to you, asking you to do for those who need shelter?

Lord help us to see You in the people and to love them as You love them. Help us to become true Ambassador's of Christ, Your treasure while we are in this world. Help people see Christ in us and help us retain the mind of Christ as we continue in our journey. Keep Your hand upon us as we walk in faith, Lord.

Become Ambassador's of Christ, God's Treasure

May we become hungry for the truth. May our Lord open the eyes of our heart so we clearly see Him and seek His truth and receive His visions for our life. Lord speak to us!

As God shared the three visions in one night with me to confirm who I am through God's eyes, may He do the same for you! May you realize how precious you are to God as your heavenly Father! May you begin to see the depth of the honor it is to be a humble servant of the most high God!

People often describe their issues and their attempts to figure it out but, months or years later they are still in the same or a similar crisis mode. As an example, it can appear my issue (the twisting and abuse of my documents / files and ID) has gone on without relief. It often feels like that but, feelings lie. Seeing people through God's eyes is a blessing! God's assignments are life-altering and that's really good. God cares. God's plans are that we might have life AND have it more abundantly, so we might prosper in what we do!

The people may never know your name but, they felt God's love when you gave them shelter, extended friendship, invited them to hear the truth about God and His word, and as you remain the humble servant of the most high God, our Father will send more and more people to you for the people in this world are hurting and filled with dis-ease which needs and deserves healing. God's plan is based upon His word:

1. Become filled with faith, for God gives us a hope and a future; realizing ***It's A Faith Walk*** in life with the opportunity to be fully surrendered to God while living our life according to ***God's Storehouse Principle*** about everything, aka learning how to live per ***God's Currency,*** as God instructed us within His word,

2. Honor and follow His commandments, especially honor the Sabbath & keep it holy (aka more time with Him),

3. Receive direct counsel and be guided by the Holy Spirit, remaining in His will and not in our human will,

4. Disciple each other as God's example of us sharpening each other in the process as iron sharpens iron,

5. Stand firm, so firm before even putting on armor,

6. Put on the full armor of God and be ready,

7. Be guided by the Holy Spirit each step of the way,

8. Share a tithe of the increase of all God provides and all that God has seeded in us, skills, talents, abilities, plus options from people you know and from your resources,

9. Become the Church in your daily life and fellowship with believers within the Body of Christ, confirming to each other that we are a people set apart from the world because we are fully equipped and trained, ready to disciple!

10. <u>Restore the flow of God's Blessings</u> per ***God's Storehouse Principle***, sharing our testimonies from our rooftops (or on the internet, in music, on the radio and during TV programs, etc.) so God's people are living the abundant life available when we live aligned with ***God's Currency*** and not the currency of a nation or the world.

Chapter 4 Kingdom Business

As Jesus Taught Us To Pray (King James version):

Our Father Who Art In Heaven

Hallowed Be Thy Name

Thy Kingdom Come

Thy Will Be Done

On Earth

As It Is In Heaven

Give Us This Day Our Daily Bread

And Forgive Us Our Debts

As We Forgive Our Debtors

And Lead Us Not Into Temptation

But Deliver Us From Evil (the Evil One)

For Thine Is The Kingdom

And The Power

And The Glory

For Ever

Amen

Never have I been able to sing this song without a lot of emotion and tears.

The depth of God's caring and promise is obvious.

God's willingness to provide all of this for us & He wants us to enjoy it and each other sharing His gifts, especially love:

Worship & Give Praise to the Father

Honoring Him in All We Do (our choices)

He Resides in Our Praises

His Kingdom Business to be Done

His Will to be Done

Then, it shall become for us on Earth

As It Is In Heaven

God's Provision

Forgiving Transgressions, Debts (full cycle)

Asking & Giving Forgiveness + Forgiving Ourselves

Repenting; Living daily life with a clear slate

As in Jabez's Prayer ... with Forgiveness, our Territory expands and we desire to remain separate from evil!

For God is our God and we seek His Will, Kingdom

And Power

And Glory

For Ever!

Amen

Kingdom Business Operates Blessing to Blessing
Glory to Glory
World-based Budget Plan is Very Different
What?

2 Corinthians 3:7-18. Glory of the New Covenant

But if the ministry of death, written *and* engraved on stones, was glorious, so that the children of Israel could not look steadily at the face of Moses because of the glory of his countenance, which *glory* was passing away, [8] how will the ministry of the Spirit not be more glorious? [9] For if the ministry of condemnation *had* glory, the ministry of righteousness exceeds much more in glory. [10] For even what was made glorious had no glory in this respect, because of the glory that excels. [11] For if what is passing away *was* glorious, what remains *is* much more glorious.

[12] Therefore, since we have such hope, we use great boldness of speech— [13] unlike Moses, *who* put a veil over his face so that the children of Israel could not look steadily at the end of what was passing away. [14] But their minds were blinded. For until this day the same veil remains unlifted in the reading of the Old Testament, because the *veil* is taken away in Christ. [15] But even to this day, when Moses is read, a veil lies on their heart. [16] Nevertheless when one turns to the Lord, the veil is taken away. [17] Now the Lord is the Spirit; and where the Spirit of the Lord *is*, there *is* liberty.

Verse 18. But we all, with unveiled face, beholding as in a mirror the glory of the Lord, are being transformed into the same image from glory to glory, just as by the Spirit of the Lord.

Kingdom Business vs. World Busy-ness

God's Currency is not the process of merely going from the process of buying products and services to bartering products and services, it is a 100% shift in our thinking and doing from world structure to Kingdom structure.

There is an **exchange** but it is not based upon world currency.

In the exchange, aka what God has 'in store for us' vs the world's offer, we are to align with God and do what we see and hear our Father do as Christ confirmed the process.

The typical exchange happens when we are aligned with God's will and it is confirmed by the Holy Spirit as the assignments are unfolding and so often it is 'not about us' because God's focus is for to speak life to the people.

It is not about 'good works' or 'kind deeds'.

The best way to visualize it is by <u>seeing us as the very extension of God's hands on earth</u> so all who fellowship in His name are blessed and none shall leave the assembly or have to live their life per the world, aka in lack or in need.

Example: A car when there is no way to buy a car.

I did not re-establish my life or arrange for an auto during the three years of ***It's A Faith Walk!*** when God took my hand. Upon my return, I was very involved helping with several issues a fellow Nebraskan was experiencing. Then I began helping with issues his parents were dealing with since his mother had muscular dystrophy. At this time, I was renting cars and praying for God's provision for car & gas.

<u>At midnight</u>, God awakened the father and told him, ***"She has done so much for you and your family, you should buy her a $_____ car."*** God provided a specific dollar amount, but the exact amount does not matter.

I checked with dealerships who honor broker rates (about $600-$900 above factory invoice to prepare the car once it arrives). The exact car was available for the dollar amount God stated.

However, to include a CD player within an 'upgrade package' to help retain a higher value for the car over time, the dealer price increased to $3,500 above the amount God stated. I told the salesman I needed to pray.

At midnight, the dealership received a fax from the corporate office and they were offering a $3,500 rebate for autos sold within the next few days.

This was so like God to exactly match the amount for the deal. Since this deal was exactly what God offered, I arranged to meet my friend's father at the dealership.

The papers were prepared for the purchase. Then, the man said he did not have the cash with him to purchase.

So, the finance officer changed the paperwork to be a loan purchase and he told my friend's father the amount for the down payment. Since he did not have cash with him, the finance officer said he would change the deal to a lease.

My friend's father signed the lease documents as the responsible party. My signature was required as the driver and insurance holder for the vehicle. Then, the finance officer said the deal was done. Due to my friend's father needing to return home to relieve the health care worker for his wife, and since the three full sets of finance paperwork at the dealership took hours vs. minutes, he left.

The dealership provided a van to follow me to the rental car agency so I could drop off my rental car. Upon my return, the finance officer said as soon as I pay the Department of Motor Vehicle fees & sales tax he will hand me the car keys.

God and I 'shared a moment'.

It was an absolutely priceless moment!

I was only at the dealership because my friend's father was supposed to be buying me a car. I did not ask for it. God had confirmed it to him, not me! So, what gives?

Well, God quickly took over. He prompted me to call the branch of my bank to confirm the amount for the dealership even though I knew I did NOT have the amount (a few thousand dollars) required to pay the fees and taxes.

God knew what I did not know. Again, a priceless moment! The amount required was available in my bank account. I was able to obtain direct confirmation from the bank branch for the finance officer so the bank would release the funds and the car keys would be released to me.

You know me well enough and how I am with God by now ***(It's A Faith Walk & God's Storehouse Principle)*** to know I did NOT let God off the hook in that moment!

Sometimes, human minds get stuck in one gear at times.

God had just arranged for documents to be signed for me to have a car.

God had clearly, miraculously arranged for the required funds to be in my checking account to cover the fees & taxes.

However, I was still in my 'upset' about the way I thought it should have taken place!

While I was expressing my rather heated upset about the man not buying the car for me even though he knew he was supposed to buy the car for me and the purchase was the very reason he was meeting me at the dealership (yes, this is how I am with God before he says breathe!), God stopped me cold in a split second when He simply asked, ***"Did man buy you that car or did I buy you that car?"***

God did not name names.

God gave His message the universal scope.

Did the world / man provide, or did God provide?

Wow. God keeps it simple!

I just have to keep reminding myself to 'think simple'!

Because of what God did in that moment, I had a car!

God knew I was unable to function in America so I could not sign documents to drive the car off the lot or have funds to pay DMV & taxes due to what I was experiencing 'in the natural' but. God **exchanged** the limits in the world when God stepped in and made it happen!

Tears flowed while I thanked God for His provision the rest of the way home (dealership with the special offer was an hour's drive from my home), and through that night …

God 'exchanged' my assistance with the family of my friend for **a promise of an auto!**

God 'exchanged' my world financial debacle (the web of deceit agents entangled me in which caused the repeated appearance of issues) for **His provision of an auto!**

I'm still driving it. People cannot believe it. They think 'it looks brand new' inside and out. It does!

I've learned to honor God's provision!

Example: God got an earful from me after I extended in London to help the High Commissioner, the Ambassador of The Kingdom of Tonga because I was to receive a blessing beyond a flight ticket to America.

But, after I prepared her for the Global Economic Summit she told me her office did not have the funds in the budget to purchase the promised flight ticket or provide a blessing.

Stuck!

She did assure me that God would provide for His servant and I could stay in her home in the meantime.

Not happy!

At midnight, I was finally exhausted from marching and praying and 'being so Sheila God had to be laughing' and I ended my tirade with:

Lord, you are my travel agent and I'm going to bed while you work it out!

Before 8 AM the phone rang. Staff ran up to the guest floor (third floor) to tell me I had a call.

At midnight, God woke a business man up. God told him the least he could do is purchase a flight ticket for what he had learned when I preached the previous Sunday.

He was calling before eight due to his tight schedule. He wanted to work out the details because he had to be in a meeting by 8 AM. His travel agent said a round-trip would be the best option with at least a seven day advance.

God 'exchanged' His information / wisdom for a ticket.

God 'exchanged' my upset regarding the 'reality in the natural' with His orchestration of all details and He arranged within the 'exchange' for me to attend a 7-day Spiritual Warfare Conference, do warfare with a Voodoo Princess ***(It's A Faith Walk!)*** which introduced me to a dozen pastors.

God Orchestrates God's Plan(s)

God Builds A Great Church / Ark / Family Lineage

I was privileged to hear a pastor from Bogota, Columbia speak about his upset with God.

He met with people in his home for five years. A few different members of the eight families have attended at various times but, the 'home church' is still the same eight families after five years of effort extended every Sunday.

He was done.

He told God that He can have His church back!

God merely said, ***"Good. You forgot that it was My church. Now see what I do with it."***

Two Sunday services due to filling a 60,000 seat stadium for 1st service; Youth service on Saturday night & Women on Wednesday evenings. **We serve an awesome God!**

Chapter 5 Kingdom Funds

Kingdom Business / Kingdom Funds

Everything God provides is to be honored.

I shared a brief note about a widow within ***God's Storehouse Principle,*** a woman God introduced me to. She was well cared for through her husband's estate plus a substantial monthly income.

She gave a $35,000 grand piano to the church in her husband's memory since the church did not have a piano and she loved piano music. The church sold the piano for about half the amount and used the funds for their monthly budget. It only helped them pay bills for a couple of months and then the church was 'in need' of a financial injection once again.

The sad part is: *The amount she paid for the piano would have been a good down payment for a very nice home or it would have purchased a home and possibly a used auto 'free and clear' for a family in need within many regions in the world, even in America.*

God Knows How We Handle Kingdom Business Funds

We have to be cautious about the flow of all resources and blessings within the cycle of ***God's Storehouse Principle*** and ***God's Currency!*** It is God's, not ours.

When we do not seek God's counsel first and follow the steps laid out before us, we may fall for or into the traps / snares in the world. ***Lord keep Your hand upon us!***

The plans God has for us are to prosper us!

The world wants us to make lemonade from lemons!

World Credit is Not Credit, It is Debt

We make choices based upon our plans, our free will and when we do not align with God's will or check with God to see if it is the best option for us. There's an old saying which fits this scenario: ***"If you did not ask God about the car before you bought it, why do you complain to God and ask God to fix it when you find out it's a lemon?"***

World Financial Structure is Upside-down

A basic currency lie: Credit being built per the world plan **in truth** equals increased debt!

We were not to become debtors.

Armed with God's truth, we can do better!

The world created the 'credit score plan' so we would think we are building high levels of credit, but this is **the lie** because it is NOT credit, it is debt and in using the option extended within the world plan we become deeply indebted. Did you know that spending more than 50% of the debt, disguised as credit, also lowers your credit score?

If you are wondering, ***"How can I pay off the debt?"*** I'm not meaning to sound cliché about this, but the quickest answer is:***Tithe / schedule more personal time with God!***

1 Kings 2:3 (NIV)

... and observe what the LORD your God requires: Walk in his ways, and keep his decrees and commands, his laws and requirements, as written in the Law of Moses, so that you may prosper in all you do and wherever you go,

Psalm 1:3

And he shall be like a tree planted by the rivers of water, that brings forth his fruit in his season; his leaf also shall not wither; and whatsoever he does shall prosper.

Romans 13:7-9 (NIV)

Give everyone what you owe him: If you owe taxes, pay taxes; if revenue, then revenue; if respect, then respect; if honor, then honor.

2 Kings 4:7 (NIV)

She went and told the man of God, and he said, *"Go, sell the oil and pay your debts. You and your sons can live on what is left."*

Deuteronomy 15

"At the end of *every* seven years you shall grant a release *of debts*. [2] And this *is* the form of the release: Every creditor who has lent *anything* to his neighbor shall release *it;* he shall not require *it* of his neighbor or his brother, because it is called the Lord's release. [3] Of a foreigner you may require *it;* but you shall give up your claim to what is owed by your brother, [4] except when there may be no poor among you; for the Lord will greatly bless you in the land which the Lord your God is giving you to possess *as* an inheritance — [5] only if you carefully obey the voice of the Lord your God, to observe with care all these commandments which I command you today. [6] For the Lord your God will bless you just as He promised you; you shall lend to many nations, but you shall not borrow; you shall reign over many nations, but they shall not reign over you.

God Wants Us To Become Set Apart From The World

God's plans are not based upon the currency of any nation or on any currency in the world.

God confirmed this again and again as we traveled the world together. I had no idea what the currency exchange rate was going to be in any nation God sent me to but, God did. He orchestrated the exact amount needed in the very moment it was required. This was done for every step of the journey, whether it was for flight tickets or hotel stays or transportation within nations or connections for the next phase of the assignment. God's orchestration was perfect!

God Does Not Live By Our Currency We Are To Live By God's Currency

Long after I should have realized the lesson with God providing the exact amount needed exactly when it was needed,

God provided a simple and precise example: God sent me to London seven times during a 12-month period. I noticed that each time I left America I had a $5 bill in my wallet & each time I returned, I still had the $5 bill in my wallet.

I thought it was strange, so I asked God about it. God clearly confirmed it was His plan every time we traveled. God confirmed he was showing me that I was living by His currency and not mine.

God was providing the need by orchestrating the details to send me nation to nation and He confirmed the exact provision while I was on the soil in every nation. God had already proven to me that I was traveling / living based upon His currency and not the currency of a nation in the world.

God's 'exchange' when we are obedient. Even though I thought I knew the process, I was very concerned one Sunday morning: I had a specific $20 American bill to buy gas at a cash station after the service. God wanted me to give the $20 to the speaker. I resisted but, God insisted. '**In exchange' for the $20,** the speaker handed me an envelope with a ministry brochure. I opened the envelope and found a new, crisp $20 bill. I asked the speaker if he accidentally dropped some money into the envelope but, he had no idea what I was talking about.

Due to **God's 'exchange'** and orchestration of the details, I can absolutely confirm we need to learn how to hear God's voice to restore each other ***(God's Storehouse Principle)*** as we are individually the church and restoration vs. revival is God's plan and message for us!

Christ is in our hearts! We are not dead. We are & Christ is alive. Our hearts do not need to be revived! Instead, we need to be 'individually' restored. This should happen each time we fellowship for we know Christ is in the midst.

God was specific within the vision shared ***(In Search of Wigglesworth*** within ***It's A Faith Walk!).***

God showed me how deeply He is concerned about us and He cares that we comprehend His plan, especially during these critical days in our history.

The vision was at the entrance to the Emergency Room of a large hospital.

The ambulances were everywhere.

Each ambulance driver opened the doors to reveal churches (identical, white wooden churches) all flat-lined (dead) wanting to be revived.

God wants us to remain close with Him, know His truth and gain His wisdom in the moment required so we know Him and we experience His truth and we see His miracles and share testimonies of His provision, healing & blessings.

In the process, our faith is renewed and strong so we can share our faith and our testimonies with all who have ears to hear and eyes to see. The world will know who we are!

The best way I can explain it: **Giving God's blessings to others increases my energy and faith. The more I give away, the more I have to give away! Full Cycle Living: The Cycle of *God's Currency!***

Due to being influenced by the world, taking on the battles the world <u>inserts</u> into God's plans for our lives, our hearts need to open to Christ to be restored so the Body of Christ will be restored. Then, after we are restored and filled with faith we are ready to live, really live!

This is why God wants us to know how to live according to ***God's Storehouse Principle*** so we will see the truth for ourselves and when we do, we will participate in the flow of blessings being restored throughout our region. As the people are discipled, equipped and trained to do the same we will become a people set apart, not depending upon the world-based currencies.

We will only depend upon ***God's Currency.***

Bottom line: When the world decides to change the rules or the nation or world decides to collapse the currency of a nation or re-value the currency so it has little or no value it will NOT matter to us for we will be members of one body operating in one accord, sharing the blessings and resources living separate and set apart from the world!

On that note, feel free to take a moment, get up and stretch.

Then, do me a favor and take a big, deep breath.

Make it a special, deep breath you take in from God, with God, and then let out aka exhale all of the old world kind of stuff that was just filling up space within you.

Over time, we have been filled with a lot of junk / lies. You need extra room now for your extra ordinary life because you are taking in a lot of truth and God's truth needs space for you to be filled with faith and to breathe in each breath of life!

When you are ready, I'll meet you at Chapter 6.

Chapter 6 God's miracle '...in the nick of time'

Do you know the story of the two frogs?

They fell into a vat of cream. Not the special blend kind to help them have better looking skin, just some plain cream.

It was hard for them to function since they had no idea where they were or what the substance was because all they knew was it was something that was definitely heavier than water and it was a different color than the muddy water they were used to. That is all they knew.

They were swatting with all four legs going full speed in their attempts to keep from sinking.

The first frog was getting tired. He did not see any progress. So, he started telling the second frog that he was thinking about giving up and giving in to the thick stuff. This would mean that he would sink and therefore, drown.

The second frog was doing all he could to encourage the first frog to keep on trying. He said that together they could figure out the problem. The first frog did not respond. The second frog realized the first frog gave up & drowned.

Then, the second frog was getting really tired. He reached a point where he felt there was no hope but, he quickly did everything he could to re-encourage himself.

He thought about the good memories of his life while all four of his legs were so tired they each wanted to give up.

To his amazement, because he kept on keepin' on, his legs churned the cream into butter. He was able to walk out.

He remained steadfast. He witnessed a miracle!

Remember: When & where we are weak, God is strong!

God wants us to know the truth and live it so we will be strong in faith, grounded in the truth and stand firm no matter what the world decides to do for the world plans are to steal, kill and destroy. However, when we learn to turn around the enemies attempts to instill fear, doubt and unbelief, we will be able to remain steadfast and aligned with God's plan and will for our life! Then, the enemy's plans cannot phase us!

Lord help us stand firm and not lose faith & hope!

God wants us to be prepared should the world change the plan tonight. These are critical days. The world economy is in crisis. National currencies are in crisis. The world has a plan for a one world structure, as defined in **Revelation 13: 15-17.** ... *cause as many as would not worship the image of the beast to be killed.* [16] *He causes all, both small and great, rich and poor, free and slave, to receive a mark on their right hand or on their foreheads,* [17] *and that no one may buy or sell except one who has the mark or the name of the beast, or the number of his name.*

We are to be ready when the time comes!

Are You Ready?

A special couple, singers I have mentioned before, Kirk & Joni Bovill, write & arrange their music. A special song / album of this title asks if we are ready, is our house in order?

We are to live 'in the world' but we are not to be 'of the world' for our God is available to us and will be with us, confirming His truth for us so we will learn how to live our life based upon ***God's Currency*** for it is what will sustain us!

Lord, we want to witness Your signs & miracles!

So often, the world pushes so hard against the dreams and plans God has for us ... that eye has not seen and ear has not heard and mind has not conceived God's plan for us ... and, we get tired being human, not realizing that we are merely tired of pushing our thoughts and viewpoints. ***God speak to us for we are tired but, we desire to serve you.***

Count It All Joy

The Enemy Knows God's Hand Is Upon You!

Sad, and yet, we do consider giving up. I pray you will remain steadfast like the second frog, the one who walks out of the problem in the world & keeps walking forward in faith!

Many times people do give up just before the miracle because the very darkest moment is often the exact moment the miracle is ready to be confirmed. **Do not give up!**

If we were not that close, the enemy would not care what was going on. Since the enemy wants to steal, kill and destroy, plus instill fear, doubt and unbelief in you, the effort of the enemy is much stronger just before the miracle is to take place! It is as though the legions of demons line up to become a huge roadblock to your blessing.

Remember: God is with you; Count It All Joy!

The Storm Is Passing Over

This is one of my favorite worship songs. It is important to realize the storms do come and they last for a short time. They do not go on and on and on. **They move on!**

Do NOT give up when the enemy pushes so hard against you. Shift your focus to God. Keep your thoughts on His promises. The miracle is not visible yet but, it is very close!

In the weakest moment, it is critical to remember God will be our strength and He will not forsake us.

Standing firm upon the truth, God's promises, until the miracle appears 'in the natural' is what we are here to do!

James 1:2-8. Profiting from Trials

My brethren, **count it all joy** when you fall into various trials, [3] knowing that the testing of your faith produces patience. [4] But **let patience have its perfect work**, that **you may be perfect and complete, lacking nothing**. [5] If any of you lacks wisdom, let him **ask of God, who gives to all liberally and without reproach**, and it will be given to him. [6] But let him **ask in faith, with no doubting, for he who doubts is like a wave of the sea driven and tossed by the wind**. [7] For l**et not that man suppose that he will receive anything from the Lord**; [8] ***he is* a double-minded man, unstable in all his ways.**

God orchestrates so much for me and He will for you!

He was doing it all for me prior to the day He confirmed everything was prepared for me. He continued to arrange everything during the unique three year journey and to this day.

God knew I needed to learn, to be equipped and trained by Him for it was clear that I could do nothing in the world after experiencing the repeated, devastating circumstances.

Part of God's training, about seven months, is what I've shared in ***It's A Faith Walk!***

The biggest lesson after learning how to walk in faith was ***God's Storehouse Principle*** a message God shared through me each time He orchestrated an invitation for me to preach. I was learning to comprehend ***God's Currency.*** It was the simple message God shared after the 7 trips to London in 12 months: ***"I do not operate based upon your currency. You are learning to live by My currency."*** I thought he was just teaching me. However, God wants the Body of Christ to know this truth.

He was showing me His currency from the very first moment. I did not see it like He did. Flight tickets were at will call, tunics were provided within each nation, introductions happened without my resume or participation, He spoke to the people in their language through me & filled the empty gas tank and kept it full for hundreds of miles, etc., etc., etc.

God clearly confirmed with each detail He orchestrated on my behalf that it has always been His plan to train each of us through His word how we are to proceed, so we know how to live, to disciple and participate in daily discipleship, share our testimonies as we disciple each other, exactly as He guides us to sharpen each other as iron sharpens iron.

Every detail God orchestrated was another example of how He was proving to me that I travel / live based upon His currency and not the currency of a nation in the world or a world-based currency. Due to God's orchestration of details and provision in many nations, I can confirm we need to learn how to live according to ***God's Currency***, because it will be what we can depend upon when the world currency (currencies) collapse. And, that is the plan in the world.

Speaking the Testimony

As confirmed in Matthew, John, and II Corinthians, we are to share the testimony and with two or three witnesses establish the truth of the testimony, and stand firm upon the truth until we witness the miracle.

We do experience miracles but we do not always testify to the miracle. It takes practice!

It is often easier to see a miracle happening for someone else and share it. We need to focus on sharing the miracle / testimony in our life with two or three witnesses and continue the sharing of our miracles for all to hear the truth!

Example: A dear friend and prayer partner was dealing with a growth in her throat. It was a major irritant and it caused her to repeatedly try and clear her throat.

Doctors confirmed the truth with a report: tumor.

She got a second opinion which confirmed: tumor.

She proclaimed the medical procedure to remove the tumor on her Facebook page, in emails and calls.

Until we have man's / the world's report, we do not have the evidence 'in hand' to share with witnesses regarding our miracle when it happens. Be sure to gather the evidence!

Beyond the Doctor / world report we sought God's report.

She returned to the doctor's office the week prior to surgery. The doctors confirmed the same truth, again: tumor. They set the exact time for the surgery.

When she arrived for the surgery, the doctor performed one more examination before beginning the procedure.

He could not find the tumor. He only saw a red spot where it used to be connected. When he told her he was not finding the tumor, she said: ***"My throat felt warm and then I thought I felt a small explosion. Could that have been the tumor?"*** The doctor was amazed. He had no idea where the pieces of the tumor would be for it was a solid mass. It was not something she would be able to swallow but, there was no evidence of the tumor he confirmed the previous week.

Share The Testimony Of The Miracle

Isaiah confirmed to share it from the rooftop, but that was the only way they could communicate to the region. As soon as we become aware of the miracle, we need to proclaim the truth and provide the evidence to two or more witnesses so it will be established in the fellowship. Then, proclaim the truth to the world, declaring who God is for us & all who love Him!

Declare the Truth

God's plan is more efficient and His promises confirm an abundant life and that we will prosper are true.

God's Currency is an efficient and prosperous process!

When we share a tithe of our increase from God's provision, we confirm a testimony of ***God's Currency.***

When we share a tithe of all that God has seeded in us, His wisdom and truth, plus our skills, talents, abilities and resources He seeded in us, we are seeding into lives throughout the region and the testimonies shall increase and spread across the land. Again, it's ***God's Currency.***

Plus, we are discipling by example. Our testimonies help fill the people with faith, encourage them to do all God has need of them to do. Then, they begin to experience ***God's Currency:*** not burdened by the 'lack' of knowledge, understanding & provision.

Over time, they become discipled, equipped and trained to do the same.

Turn the Tide with Truth
You Will Begin to See Life being
Breathed into the Fellowship

Sharing Truth / Testimonies & Expanding The Territory Knowing What to Do When the Evil One Attempts to Change The Plan, but Evil Runs When You Establish a Firm Foundation with Witnesses

Individually, as we gather and fellowship, we are the church the Body of Christ. Over time the church body became heavily dependent upon the world, the national / world's currency. **We can change this starting today!**

Over time, the people became more and more dependent upon the world's plan, the world's currency, the government programs and the rules and regulations of the world's programs which are directing the people regarding how they are to live their life.

This status can and will change as soon as we realize in our heart and mind the big plans God has for us.

We do NOT have to accept this status as the 'norm' for we can turn this tide, capture the vision God has for our lives and as joint heirs we will pass the inheritance on to the 3rd and 4th generations.

We can do better knowing what God planned for us.

We were formed in God's image. We can do better!

Those who have been left to depend upon the government programs include far more than the widows and orphans. In the current generations, entire families are on the government programs or living homeless.

There is much for us to do to turn the tide!

We can speak to this mountain and when we do, it will have to move!

We are here to help it be on earth as it is in heaven.

We can become a force for the enemy to have to reckon with!

Lord forgive us for we knew not what we did!

Chapter 7 Prepare: Set Apart From The World

If we were living our life based upon God's Currency, as though we truly are the Church / the Body of Christ, it would not matter if the national or world-based currency crashed because we would not be affected.

Due to the current status of the global economy, I wish the body of Christ was already operating based upon ***God's Currency.***

God does not refer to cash amounts calculated for barters, God provided the structure as outlined within the Bible so we would have life abundantly and prosper on the land by proceeding as He commanded (briefly outlined within ***God's Storehouse Principle),*** by realizing God provided it all and we are here not only to enjoy it but, share a tithe of all that He has seeded in us and of the increase He has provided to us. We then become a blessing while God counsels us so we know what to do for all to be blessed.

We need to prepare as God's people, set apart from the world, sharing and enjoying all God has provided with all who have ears to hear and eyes to see so we do not have to take the mark to buy & sell. We are to prepare so we do not need anything from the world's marketplace!

The world plan is clearly outlined in **Revelations 13:16-17a.** *It also forced all people, great and small, rich and poor, free and slave, to <u>receive a mark on their right hands or on their foreheads,</u>* *[17] <u>so that they could not buy or sell unless they had the mark</u>* ...

With God's wisdom 'in hand' we will be prepared when the day arrives and we are given the choice to take the mark if you want to purchase or sell anything in the marketplace.

We need to prepare.

Sharing these details to inform you and help you prepare, not to cause you to become fearful for we are to stand firm in faith and we wise as the serpent and yet remain as gentle as a dove. Some churches have contacted me about preparing concrete bunkers. We are not to live in fear. We are to become the example.

Free Will, Free Choice

When we make a choice or a stack of choices which align with our free will vs. God's will, we can find ourselves in a situation which we want to get out of and even though our choices got us into a tough point in our life. We need to be sure we are aligned with God so He will know us and answer our cry to **exchange** 'what the world plans for us' with the plan God has 'in store' for us who love Him.

Praying We Have Enough Time to Wake Up the Church

We are in need of God's assistance in this hour. Currencies of most nations are in jeopardy. Allowing man to control the banking system and the currency rates was known to be a problem before America was established.

In America, the forefathers knew the problems caused by a centralized bank in England. They established the banking structure in America in a different structure so it would not happen in America.

Thomas Jefferson. In the debate over the *Re-charter of the Bank Bill* (1809): ***If the American people ever allow private banks to control the issue of their currency*** (centralized bank, Federal Reserve Notes vs. dollars), ***first by inflation, then by deflation, the banks...will deprive the people of all property until their children wake-up homeless on the continent their fathers conquered.... The issuing power should be taken from the banks and restored to the people, to whom it properly belongs.***

The currency was always strong in America due to being backed by gold. American currency was always the "reserve currency" since it was solid due to being backed by gold. But, it was removed from the gold standard and for the first time in history it has not been returned to the gold standard.

Lord Forgive Us For We Knew Not What We Did

Lord Forgive Us For We Knew Not What We Allowed

Lord Help Us, Keep Your Hand Upon Us

This is the hour!

What if this is our 'one moment in time' to stand firm and re-align with God's plan for our life to be lived abundantly so we become God's church the true Body of Christ and we are not affected by the currencies of the world or a nation?

It is possible!

Lord Help Us Align To Your Will, Your Purpose & Plan

Have you experienced the 'saving grace of God' which happens in a split second, in the blink of an eye, or in some cases in the eleventh hour or perhaps closer to 11:30?

In that moment God steps in, shows up mightily, and **exchanges** the world plan for your life with His plan.

God Confirms Life vs. Death
A Moment in Time Becomes the Difference
Between Life and Death!

I shared two specific examples within ***God's Storehouse Principle.***

First example: God wanted me to call a dear friend who had not been in communication or answered a call or an email in several days. When I called, I reached the voice mail. I wanted to hang up but, God wanted me to leave a message. He wanted me to tell her, "***God is giving you a new song.***" God told me to give her this same message three times. I did not hear from her for a few days but, when she called she was in tears. She was so sick, she could not lift her head or breathe deep enough to lift the receiver or speak a word. She was near the phone and she heard my voice through the voice mail system. She was in tears as she heard the words. They were a direct answer to prayer.

Moments before my call she cried out to God to know if she was dying. Since she used to be a singer, she made a deal with God. She told Him if she was not dying He needed to send three confirmations that He was giving her a new song. She wanted to laugh when she realized how quickly God sent the three confirmations within the one prayer I prayed. She could not do anything beyond thank God from her heart and go into a deep rest with God while He healed her and continued to fill her with His breath of life and plans.

God gave her a miracle and extended her life!

Second example: God wanted me to call a dear prayer partner in the exact moment which caused her to realize she was unable to form words let alone state a phrase that made any sense.

She needed to arrange to go to the hospital. I was trying to do everything possible over the phone which would save her the costs of going to the hospital but, I did not receive a separate message from God. I was only prompted to call her and per God's prompting in that exact moment she became aware of the fact she was experiencing a stroke.

She did go to the hospital. She found out from the Doctor's that her blood pressure was so high she should have been dead. Ah, the comforting words of the Doctors!

But, God … in the moment of need … directly provided her with the truth and then sustained her and continued to breathe life into her until she reached the hospital and heard the facts about her health condition.

Per the Doctor's confirmation, she had already lived well beyond what human comprehension could understand based upon the facts of how quickly a stroke progresses.

God has plans for her.

God gave her a miracle and extended her life!

God's Plans are Life, not Death!

God's Word is Truth, not Lies!

God's plans for us are life, not death; truth, not lies; blessings flowing believer to believer keeping the body of Christ filled to overflowing with powerful testimonies to encourage each member to keep on keepin' on by faith.

When the Pastor is Away

I received a call from a dear pastor friend in California. He was devastated. He could not preach the next Sunday so he asked me to come and preach.

It had been a special time for him since the church sent him to Hawaii on a late honeymoon (35th wedding anniversary) due to not being able to go on a honeymoon when they were married.

It was their first 'couple' vacation since they were married.

When he returned, his assistant informed him that while he was away the associate pastor told the people the Lord wanted him to start a new congregation with 50 families from the church. The people proceeded because they were told the Lord directed the plan.

My concern: What do you want me to say Lord?

As God often works with me, I did not receive a message until I was in the church on Sunday morning.

God told me to take the microphone in my hands and place my hands around the microphone, so I did.

God wanted me to close my hands around the microphone and speak into the dark. This was the first key.

Then, God told me to open my mouth. When I did, God said: ***"While the pastor is away, tell the people in his church you are supposed to take fifty of the families and start your own church. Do not tell the pastor. Do it before the pastor returns."***

Then, God merely had me tell the people how to distinguish between God's plan / voice and the world / enemy plan. God made it simple: **God operates in the open / truth and not in the dark / lies.**

When the Cupboard is Bare

I was munching on the last carrots in the fridge. They were old but, they were there so I ate them. Then, I got sick.

I needed encouragement. When I started to feel a little better, I called a prayer partner.

He told me when they were out of food and everything they needed for their two baby girls his wife dressed in her best dress, laid down on the bed and waited for Jesus to take her home. This was not sounding encouraging!

But, in that moment, the doorbell rang. A woman was at the door with bags of groceries. God told her to buy each item at the store, including the right diaper sizes for the two baby girls in the brand they preferred.

He said he would pray while he trusted the same thing would happen for me.

I was 'having a chat with God' and not feeling encouraged. I did not put on my best dress and lay down but, within a moment I heard the doorbell ring.

A woman stopped by to pick me up because some women were gathering together to go to a Rodney Howard Browne meeting and they wanted me to go with them.

God prompted me to grab some of the scarves I sell when I speak. That night women purchased the scarves. I received exactly the amount needed to provide a blessing as an abundant tip when we stopped to eat and fellowship together and to buy what I would need for the next journey, and rent a car to take me to the airport. I did not need anything else since any food purchased would spoil due to God already orchestrating the next trip!

God stepped in and **exchanged** the view I had of my situation with a brand new view from His perspective, plus God provided exactly enough to meet the needs and send me on the next assignment.

Only God knows 'in advance' what is being divinely orchestrated on our behalf! His plans bless the people in our life, the multitude. All we have to do is be patient, remember

When God Needs Us

God arranges all details in the nick of time, also known as (aka) eleventh hour. His orchestration is beyond human options!

Australia in three days; call the airlines. Hotel in Australia; stop by the PO Box before the flight to pick up a check.

Rental car agency changes policy to require $200 deposit when I only had $40 cash 'in hand'; go to the PO Box for a check to cover the balance: $164.50. Hopeful of the $4.50 balance to purchase some fruit and vegetables but, the manager kept the check; go to a friend's home and check emails; flight arranged the next morning without options to buy a ticket; go to the will call window at the airport. Friend shared a meal and if I would have purchased food it would be wasted as I did not need anything before the next journey. **I may not know God's plans but, God has plans!**

The list goes on & on & on & on with a few of the details shared in I***t's A Faith Walk*** and ***God's Storehouse Principle***, plus, I am inserting a few as more reminders because God's desire is to be with each of us in the moment of our need and it is a universal message we need to spread across the globe.

In addition to the many confirmations of what God will do in the moment of need, God also protects me when the enemy makes a plan to steal, kill or destroy. God steps in during the exact moment when everything in the world would indicate the plan will result in a deadly situation.

Protection from Disaster on the Freeway

It was a bright sunny day and I was enjoying the coast highway route to Los Angeles. The day was so nice, I opened the sun roof of my car. The music was playing and I was unaware of the fact a man wanted his midnight blue SUV in my lane even though there was no option due to the fact the freeway was an absolute parking lot.

This often happens on the 5 Freeway as the traffic approaches the border check point.

Since he was not successful squeezing in from the lane on my right due to all cars being stopped and there was no room for him to squeeze in, he slammed on his horn and drove sideways between my car and the car behind me.

He continued his illegal plan until he was driving illegally on the shoulder of the road, evidently unaware of the fact the optional car pool lane was not open to traffic and significant barriers were closing in fast due to his speed. He was unaware of the facts which would cause him to not be successful if he wanted to squeeze in front of my car from the shoulder of the road, either.

But, nothing 'in the world' slowed his vehicle down.

Regardless of the truth, he drove his SUV into my lane of traffic. I was aware of his maneuver but, not comprehending it since it was clearly not possible for both vehicles to occupy the same space within the same lane of traffic.

God Stepped In

God stepped in and **exchanged** what would have happened (my car would have been totaled) in that exact moment in time.

Everything was in slow motion. I saw his SUV coming into my lane to take the place of my vehicle but, I was still driving my car in the lane!

No fear came over me as I felt protected while it was like watching a movie instead of being in the scene as I heard a gentle 'whoosh' sound.

Then, God prompted me to turn my head toward the SUV and I saw a deep indentation being made along the entire passenger side of his SUV, beginning at the front of his vehicle and continuing the entire length.

Due to the barriers of the car pool lane and God's help, my car was 'suspended in time' while his SUV continued through my lane and the lane on my right over to the third lane.

This was an impossible option 'in the natural' because all traffic was at a standstill. But, possible since God stepped in!

The traffic was so much slower in the third lane, evidently due to some issues with a car at the checkpoint in that lane. He did not gain anything with all of his maneuvers.

He was stuck while my lane of traffic moved forward.

As soon as I reached the border check point, I told the Border Patrol Agent what happened. He directed me to the side of the road by the Highway Patrol building and he told the Agent in the third lane about the SUV needing to pull over, also.

The Agent said my car looks fine on the driver's side. But, I was concerned about the damage to the SUV. I did not want any problems in the future with my insurance company.

When the man pulled over, he was extremely upset. He flew out of his vehicle, screamed at the Agents that he was already late for a meeting. He said he had no time to hear about (my) issue. So, even though the Agents saw the extensive damage to the passenger side of his SUV, they told him to have a nice day.

The man immediately drove away.

Again, God directed my attention to the passenger side of the SUV and I saw the deep indentation. It was very evident along the entire length of his SUV. I pointed to it as the Agents told me it is not my responsibility because I've done what I could do to bring it to the man's attention. They also said that due to the level of the man's anger I should stay clear of his vehicle during the rest of my trip. The man was long gone so it was easy to follow their advice.

God Provides The Evidence

When I arrived at the security gate of the Tribune Broadcasting Studio lot, I was at peace as I entered the beautiful, former location of Warner Brothers Studios.

My only concern: I wondered how I would be able to share the amazing testimony of what God did for me because the two witnesses were at the border check point.

God could not keep me quiet.

When I shared the first words with the studio executives about how it felt, how it was like watching while the finger of God reached down when He stepped in. The men wanted to see my car.

I was praying diligently for God's evidence of my testimony as we walked out of the building to the guest area of the studio parking lot.

To my complete surprise we saw that the outer corner of the driver's side mirror was covered with a thick, large stack of what looked like white dust.

The men were speechless and in awe when they saw the white dust. They told me the white dust is the paint dust from the SUV. So, I told them again that the SUV was midnight blue.

They said the white dust confirms the depth of the damage to the SUV since the white is under the topcoat, directly against the metal frame.

They also pointed out the layers of the paint are obvious due to the stack being a repeat of the dark blue to the white.

They were amazed to see all of the layers of the dust and that they were still visible on the tip of the mirror since I was on the freeway at least 60 miles before I entered the gates of the studio.

Lord may we be bold with our testimonies!

Currency Comes In Many Forms

When the LORD sent me to the children's home (since I've been told it is not politically correct in these days to call the orphanage an orphanage any more), He only provided the name of the young girl to pray for when I arrive.

The LORD knew she was ready to commit suicide. She did not have guidance or discipleship even though she loved the LORD and wanted to only serve him.

So, she was hearing from the enemy and believing his lies.

She was not able to gain a second chance at the school or at the home. Per the non-believing teacher, her record would remain 'as is' for the rest of the school year. The record at the school resulted in an identical stand by the administration of the children's home.

The enemy convinced her that she should go to heaven (commit suicide) and ask the LORD to become an angel with wings so she can go where she needs to go to do what she needs to do for people to be healed and have a second chance. And, the enemy added that she should negotiate with the LORD for the Nephilim to have a second chance because they have not been given a second chance.

The LORD prompted me to write the word rebellion on a napkin. Then, draw a line between the two l's. When I asked if she was in a bit of rebellion she became very shy and said, ***Yes Ma'am.***

So I asked if she really wanted to rebel against the Lion of Judah because He is Christ. She was in shock and said, ***No Ma'am.***

The enemy told her lies: the queen of heaven is Mary, the mother of Jesus and Baal is God's assistant.

Nephilim, queen of heaven and Baal were not names which were known by me at the age of 12! The enemy is working hard on the young people in these days!

I asked the young lady if we could pray together. She wanted to receive prayer. Then, she wanted to learn how to pray like I pray. Our time was limited to a two hour time slot and God made every minute count!

When I returned to the hosting home, I entered into intense prayer. At midnight, I left it all with the LORD.

The next day, I received a call about a car being donated to my ministry. A woman was awakened at midnight and told by the LORD to donate her BMW station wagon to the woman in ministry she heard about for the last nine months.

Her son was fourteen and a half and his initals are BMW. He was going to receive the car when he turned 16. So, his mother asked him to pray and see what the LORD would reveal to him. The LORD revealed the same message to him so they arranged for me to immediately receive the car.

My first question of the LORD on Thursday morning was which location should I go to first, the school or the children's home? I'll go to both.

The LORD merely said, ***I got this!***

Surprised, so I asked two more times. Trusting the LORD was not surprised because His answer remained the same!

Currency Calculator

For two hours or praying with the young lady, the LORD arranged the following:

1. The non-believing teacher was touched by the LORD. The next Sunday, the young lady said, ***On Thursday morning my non-believing teacher told me she never removes something from a student's record once it is in the record but, she's supposed to do it for me. She never gives a student a second chance but, she's supposed to do it for me ...!***
2. The administration at the children's home corrected the record and all privileges taken away were restored!
3. Mother of the young lady was out of work which was resulted in being forced to leave her daughter at the home. The young lady had changed her prayer life and taught her mother how to pray and her mother got a job two weeks after we met.
4. A BMW station wagon valued at $2,300 for two hours or prayer, was provided so I could go where He needs me to go to do what He needs me to do and say what He needs me to say.

More Currency

The LORD arranged the flight ticket for me to be in Australia within three days. He extended me in the region for seven more days, seven times!

Then, He added seven days in the Kingdom of Tonga at the end of the Australia trip which provided the opportunity to meet with and bless a pastor in Fiji, the original reason to be in the region!

Currency Calculator

1. Flight ticket to Australia, arranged ($1200).

2. Hosting for seven weeks in Australia (PRICELESS), family united after being estranged for decades (PRICELESS).

3. Families, businesses and churches in the region forever changed and testimonies shared throughout the region (PRICELESS).

4. Meeting with pastor for 24 hours in Fiji, an option which was not possible until the LORD orchestrated the trip to the Kingdom of Tonga with the flight requiring an overnight stay in Fiji (PRICELESS).

5. Flight ticket to Tonga ($1200).

6. Government closed for the day to hear the truth (PRICELESS).

7. Department heads (30) given a specific scripture during personal coaching time (MIRACULOUS and PRICELESS).

8. A nation changed with hope restored and a future re-confirmed (ETERNALLY PRICELESS).

Comprehending Currency

It is not easy to comprehend the Currency the LORD provides until we are willing to surrender to His plan, walk in Faith, function within His Storehouse and operate within His Currency!

Only the LORD can arrange tickets, send us to foreign lands, change hearts, families, how we operate as 'the church', businesses and nations and do it all without our currency, silver or gold!

I've often been told: If you are working for the LORD you would have a nice home by now, you would be driving a newer car ... He would provide for all of your bills to be paid when you are out of the country ... if you do not have everything you need, then, there is something wrong with your relationship with the LORD.

None of the criteria from 'well meaning Christians' who operate within the world based success plan relates to walking in faith with the LORD!

Not easy to hear the comments but, it opens up an opportunity to help change their heart, their mind and draw them back to the feet of Jesus!

Not easy to depart from man and follow the LORD but, it is critical to realize who's approval you are seeking, man or God?

Only the LORD can help us operate globally without an extra coin or tunic. Only He can send us to nations where the language is not known to us and yet the people understand every word.

Our LORD has proven over and over again that only one currency will help us operate anywhere in the world at any time. That currency is ***God's Currency***!

May our faith be evident and become contagious!

May the Storehouse become how we function with each other!

May the currency we learn to operate within be His currency!

Martin Luther

"The whole being of any Christian is faith and love. Faith brings the person to God, love brings the person to people."

"Faith is a living and unshakable confidence, a belief in the grace of God so assured that a man would die a thousand deaths for its sake."

"I believe that I cannot by my own reason or strength believe in Jesus Christ, my Lord, or come to Him; but the Holy Ghost has called me by the Gospel, enlightened me with His gifts, sanctified and kept me in the true faith..."

Henrietta Mears

"Faith is caught rather than taught."

Robert Louis Stevenson

"Don't judge each day by the harvest you reap, but by the seeds you plant."

Epilogue

God's Currency: It Comes In All Denominations!

Yes. Pun intended!

Some currency looks and feels great.

Some currency, well ... not so much.

Some results in tearful times. Not negative times, just tearful.

It's not always easy to see what God is doing 'in the moment when it is happening' or what the benefit will be 'in the future'. Trust is required!

God You Can Send Me ... But, You want me to stop and 'Splain it' ... in English? Me? Really?

In this experience, again, I have to trust! My very reason for being hesitant about another book: I was very sure God was NOT really tapping me on my shoulder to be the person to issue these two messages: ***God's Currency*** and ***God's Storehouse Principle.***

My concern is due to the fact I have been dealing with a long term debacle unfolding in the world. I've been beating the drum loudly, far and wide, without getting one response within the Body of Christ for any help beyond, ***"I'll pray for you."*** God knows I've needed understanding and a lot of legal wisdom plus some help.

The worldly plan that has impacted my life for more than two decades includes God's deep, deep training while I was experiencing the exact global issues God revealed to me during the days and nights of crying out for relief. There has not been a 'break' in the intense process, aka living through an additional criminal element due to experiencing the most extreme case of ID theft on record while also being a target after submitting facts regarding Superior Court judges and attorneys who were investigated by federal agents with a few being convicted on Federal RICO charges and serving prison terms. Then spending five additional years bringing the top economic fraud DA referred by the federal agents to justice. He was finally arrested, convicted and sentenced on felony fraud. As a by-product.

The financial fraud crimes within ID theft are so deeply rooted in the world plan for the New World Order. Therefore, they have so many layers which are unfolding and I was able to observe the details first hand. Each layer is directed toward unraveling the very fabric of the global economy, devastating the financial plans of the people and their families, businesses, cities and communities, and entire nations!

People often say they feel so sorry for me because the LORD has allowed all of this to happen to me but, the LORD knows the depth of who we are and all that is planned for us and He will never leave us or forsake us. Plus, He is our rear guard. So, I pressed in and continued to walk forward in faith!

But, try as I might (as the mouse to the elephant) I could not get the leadership in the Body of Christ to understand or unite and do something to turn it around.

As the woman stated prophetically to me (shared in ***It's A Faith Walk!***), ***"Even God cried."*** To know the depth of God's caring, it gave me hope! But, there was a consistent response from top leadership in the Body of Christ: ***"These are the end times. This is what is going to happen."***

Really? We are not preparing the people for anything.

We just surrender to the world plan? Really?

We just let it all happen the way the world wants it to happen and we go silent and let many perish? Really?

This has NOT been my experience with God.

God has prompted me to remain diligent!

God revealed SO MUCH & He always has a purpose!

NOT ONCE has God told me to stop beating the drum.

I told each of the leaders who dismissed any option to help the people learn how to turn the situation around, ***"Did God not say if ONE would cry out in His name?"***

I've listened to God's plan each step of the way but, while holding on by a very thin thread I've actually had a lot of people tell me I cannot sell the scarves because they are 'praise tools'. Really?

Truth: God <u>exchanged</u> the sale of the scarves for the exact need time after time.

Example: Trip to Africa.

God **<u>exchanged</u>** my purchase of scarves in time to save the lease for the business importing the scarves.

God **<u>exchanged</u>** the business purchase of scarves to fund a ministry in Korea. Full cycle of blessings!

Then, I was told ***"You cannot charge anything. That is selling ministry…it all needs to be for free."***

God would only let me say, ***"Bless you. May the Lord speak to you in your waking and resting so deeply you even hear Him when He whispers!"*** for many are not hearing God's voice! **Lord help us love as You love!**

Would the people saying this keep traveling and helping day after day 'for free'? I've often been in a position where an offering was <u>not</u> taken and I had already paid for the flight / gas to be there to bless. I'm often reminded of the saying:

Oh Lord to be with You above, now that will be the glory
But, while I'm still here below, with these saints I know
Oh Lord, that's a different story!

Trusting you are hearing & seeing why so many powerful men and women of God have stopped serving the people for there are needs God's people can fulfill upon when servants in ministry return from ministry trips.

God's Currency is based upon the flow of God's blessings one to another!

Lord help us love as You love!

May we always seek options to bless & be a blessing! May God smile when He sees who we are being while we represent Him during our time on earth!

I look forward to hearing from you regarding everything God is revealing to you as you proceed knowing ***It's A Faith Walk*** as you align with ***God's Storehouse Principle*** and operate in life within ***God's Currency.***

Until the next ONE MORE TIME our Lord brings us together, may you continue to experience HIS Best!

Sheila

Email: hisbest4usorders@gmail.com
Use the Subject Line: ***God's Currency***
Web site: http://hisbest4us.org
Facebook: HISBest4us

Ephesians 2:19-22 *We are no longer foreigners and aliens, but fellow\citizens...members of God's household, built on the foundation of the apostles and prophets, with Christ Jesus himself as the chief cornerstone. In Him the whole building is joined together and rises to become a holy temple in the Lord. And in Him you too are being built together to become a dwelling in which God lives by His Spirit.*

II Corinthians 12:14-15. (a) *"Now, I am ready to visit you...what I want is not your possessions but you...So I will very gladly spend for you everything I have and expend myself as well."*

II Corinthians 13:11-14. *Aim for perfection...be of one mind, live in peace, and the God of love and peace will be with you. May the grace of the Lord Jesus Christ, and the love of God, and the fellowship of the Holy Spirit be with you all.*

ACKNOWLEDGMENTS

AFRICA

Ghana, West Africa

Pastor Sam,

"Truly, God has sent you to us with a strong word for our church."

Pastor Charles,

" It blesses my soul to hear of your faith & see the fruit of the ministry."

Johannesburg, South Africa

Pastor Jhanni,

"God is doing a good work through you and I pray with you & our church."

Coronation Ceremony

AMERICA

Dr. Nancy Franklin, Georgia

"Thank you God for answering my prayers by sending Your apostle to (the region) to unite the believers ... "

Prophetess Nancy Haney, Alaska

"God has never given me this before. I see circles and circles and circles ... you drink and you draw from one circle to the other, and that's what you do, you drink and draw and you bring these circles together ... Pulling many groups together. All these groups need each other ... He can use you for you have ears to hear and you hear His

deep truth. You are filtering what is nonsense and what is real ... because you have been in that circle, and because of what you say they are going to merge. It is going to expand, become bigger than you could imagine."

Man of God (Georgia), Requesting to be Discipled while attending the coronation of a King in Africa, Georgia

"...at my age, it is hard to believe I am learning so much in these few days about what I did not know...realizing what it is to know that I know how it is to live within God's word each day. Will you consider discipling me?"

Pastor, Host of "Praise the Lord", TBN, **"...The fruit of the ministry is evident in your testimony..."**

International Prophet, **"You have remained steadfast to God's plan and God will continue to send you forth for His plan and purpose to be fulfilled, and for the thousands who have not knelt..."**

President, Christian Publishing Company

"Only God could orchestrate such a grand plan..."

Prayer Director, International Prayer Center

"God is opening many doors for you…"

Christian Publisher,

"God has given you a powerful voice and a sweet spirit…"

Pastor, Southern California

"God is raising you up and sending you forth to many nations…"

International Apostle

"God is doing a mighty work through you, for His righteousness precedes you, showers over you and follows you as a mighty wake. May it continue for each of your days…"

Prophetic Prayer Partner, Minnesota

"Only God could walk you through these days… accomplish so much through you, in the midst of your daily situations, the many blessings shared during each of your travels will continue to shower blessings upon each of the many households around the world…"

AUSTRALIA

Newcastle, New South Wales, Australia

Pastor Mark, "…**the staff and business leaders heard the message of Personal &Professional Life Management this week, so we are blessed you agreed to preach the word to our church this morning."**

Prayer Team "**We know now how we will we be able to continue this mighty work when you are not in our midst…"**

Four Square Gospel Church, Aboriginal Cultural Center

Pastor Rex, "**God blessed us through your preaching on Easter Sunday. We will never forget that you were in our midst ... God brought new people to Jesus today & we thank God for what He has done because you answered His call.**"

ENGLAND

London, England

Pastor Vincent, Glory House, East London,

*"...**the honor is ours this Easter Sunday.**"*

Associate Pastor,

"The Glory of our God Almighty shines upon you and through you in your speaking and your actions...we give Him praise."

Protocol Team,

"**God has mightily blessed us, by sending you into our midst.**"

Pastor Arnold,

"**You have blessed the people, and in His wisdom and timing timing, may He bring you back into our midst again, very soon.**"

Pastor, West London,

"We rejoice with you in hearing and seeing the mighty things God is doing."

Pastor, South London, **"Our God is evidenced in your life and your speaking, while we continue to thank God for the work He is doing through you..."**

High Commissioner, Kingdom of Tonga, serving in the Embassy in London, England; Ambassador, Akosita, **"God's timing is always right...for you to be with**

us, prior to the Economic Summit, to meet and pray with us..."

Sunderland, England

Anglican, Former Church of Pastor Smith Wigglesworth

Pastor Day, **"I thank God for sending you to our church this morning, for serving communion to me, and for renewing and restoring me for the call upon my life."**

Kingdom of TONGA

Pastor Isileli Taukolo, "**Our board and business leaders were fasting and praying and God confirmed He was sending someone to us. We are deeply touched by the message God sent to us, through you.**"

Minister of Finance, Tasi, "**Our meeting was an answer to my prayers, and I thank you for providing the seminar for our senior staff members, and meeting with them individually for prayer and coaching.**"

Government Office, “**Thank you for speaking today and for staying and praying with us.**”

Interpreter, Sela

Testimonials

Business to Business, Nation to Nation

B. Crousure, President
Medical Corporation

"Hiring Ms. Holm to help me structure my first business was the brightest decision I have made. She taught me how to understand what success demands of me and she trained me how to operate at her level of commitment, while expressing an intense passion for my life and for the business, and to significantly contribute to the community. Without her coaching, I know my wife, my team and I would still be standing squarely in the lackluster mire she found us in, today, instead of our business being rated on the New York Stock Exchange (NYSE). Her coaching techniques were the turning point for our lives and for our company. We have catapulted into and experienced fantastic growth, both internally and externally. We anticipated receiving help with business systems, however, her extensive experience in balancing every area of our life first, and then inserting our business into our life has made a huge difference in our life and our bottom line. Her depth of knowledge in life and corporate structuring has been the key to our success. As a lifetime athlete, I should have made the connection to what coaching would mean to my business. It has been the "play book", the two-hour training sessions, the chalk talks before the game, and the champagne after the victories!"

P. Long, Post Office Employee
United States Post Office

"Coaching is nothing like consulting! We have met with a few consultants about each of our business tasks and how the work flow should progress. However, when I attended our conference and heard about a speaker who identified specific coaching techniques which could positively impact each aspect of my life...I laughed and said, 'I will not be in that session'. Then, when I walked down the hallway, I realized something was going on, since the <u>*only*</u> *place left in the room, was an opening to lean against the wall. I'm so glad I walked in...every aspect of my life has been impacted positively, since I heard Ms. Holm speak that evening. I thank you, and my family and my co-workers thank you!"*

R. Oliver, Executive Vice President
Utility Company

"My staff had always attended the seminars, while I budgeted and selected the people to attend. However, I did not attend. I did not realize, until the first two hour session with Ms. Holm, I had always delegated the daily assignments at the office <u>*and*</u> *at home, especially when I stated that I* <u>*let*</u> *my wife adopt two daughters. We*

had help at home, I had help at the office, and all of the daily needs were met. However, I did not have a "extra" ordinary life! I did not have a meaningful relationship with anyone, including myself, until I met Ms. Holm. Nothing about my life is the same, since the first moments we met and I heard her speak about the TIME secret. I have gained an ability to relate personally to the people in my daily life. Our daughters now fight to sit closest to me. The results have been amazing, and I will always be grateful."

R. Tretsven, Owner
Beauty Supply, with Salon Services

"Prior to hearing Sheila speak, I absolutely did not have a life! I progressed through each day, each week and month, fighting to keep ahead of the bills. Each time the business level plateaued, I went into a panic, a spin, and adjusted each section of the business, ie., I would stop ordering products, or reduce the number of technicians or sales staff, or obtain a new or expanded credit line. Everything about my business, and my life, were "out of control" and "out of balance." Then, when I tried the scheduling and budgeting techniques she described, I immediately noticed an increase of 35% in business, and 100% in life."

T. Fakafanua, Minister of Finance
Kingdom of Tonga

"Within the first 30 minutes of being introduced to Sheila, I scheduled a seminar and individual coaching sessions for our top 30 department heads and Treasury Department senior staff members. The timing was perfect, as we needed to restructure our policies, procedures and the entire operating plan, within the next 30 days. Ms. Holm provided a clear and practical outline for us to use, to structure our lives, our departments, and our government"

C. Lynch, Corporate Engineering Manager
Aerospace Industry, Entrepreneur and Owner

"I would still be working on my business plan and living without a life plan, for the first business instead of owning and operating three businesses today and enjoying an "extra" ordinary life, if I had not signed up for the Entrepreneurial Course with Ms. Holm. It was immediately evident in the course, I did not have a successful plan for my day, let alone a plan for my life, my family or my business. My business ideas were innovative, as I am a successful engineer and manager. However, I was not aware of the techniques required to establish a plan for my life or for my business start-up or the required steps to ensure the success of my business through the various development phases. The practical information and the step-by-step format of the coaching and the course made it possible to 'fill in the blanks' to establish my daily life plan, to fulfill upon my plans and goals, and to proceed with a successful business plan and structure, while I was supported by the coach, and now, I can easily update my life and business plan each day! Many thanks, coach!"

J. Schneider, Vice President
Interior Design Corporation

"We not only gained your level of passion and energy for our life, we gained the same level of energy and passion for our business and everyone who contributes to it. We are excited about the many techniques we learned, to search for everyone our business can contribute to within our community! We also profited significantly from the insights which surfaced, while we were creating our business, marketing and operational plans together. Thanks for believing in us during our periods of doubt, causing us to obtain the ability to create and proceed upon dynamic personal goals and then exceed all expectations by producing results beyond our previous three and five year plans within the first project plan. We have learned to 'not dig up with doubt, the seeds we planted in faith'. Thanks for everything!"

T. Lehman, President
Furniture Manufacturing, Distribution and Sales

"The division we targeted for closure this month received our annual EXCELLENCE in Performance award for being our most improved division. Through your coaching process, causing each of us to create powerful life plans and then powerful plans for our work projects, teams automatically developed and began functioning effectively and <u>profitably</u>. The value of the staff believing in themselves far exceeds our initial intended results! The initial project resulted in a 50% increase in production and a 30% increase in related sales within the first 90 days."

International: Business Adviser & Coach

Sheila Holm advises and coaches business owners and their management teams based upon God's Storehouse Principle. God does more in the lives of the people than provide immediate, positive, bottom-line strategies. The marketing and operations strategies identified specifically for each business and industry, produce profitable, long-term results. Sheila's clients track and report 30-230% increases, based upon their first working session. Her marketing focus on co-inventing the future of each business, evokes internal and external partnerships to immediately be identified and developed. With her dynamic leadership, each staff member and customer immediately recognize the changes in the business and they commit to expand their role in working in partnership with the business and the owner and team. Then, her ability to ignite dialogue and inquiry throughout the business, immediately causes leadership to emerge within the business and each partnership (i.e., with each staff member and customer) and expand into powerful business relationships.

Credentialed: Entrepreneurial Trainer, Seminar Leader, University Instructor & Educator

Ms. Holm was awarded an American federal contract to provide entrepreneurial training for executives within both the defense and aerospace industries where she trained engineers and top management from General Dynamics, Hughes, and Lockheed. The successful training program evolved into a copyrighted, credentialed, entrepreneurial training course. Ms. Holm established a panel of industry leaders to provide a management certificate program within the California University system and she is a recognized, international seminar leader. Recently, she conducted a seminar for 30 senior staff members within the Treasury Department of the Kingdom of Tonga and she became the advisor to the Minister of Finance and to The High Commissioner (Ambassador) of Tonga, in London, while preparing for the Global Economic Summit.

Keynote Conference Speaker, TV and Radio Celebrity, and Author

*Sheila has provided the keynote address for various professional associations and corporations. She is known for her "**Balanced Life Game"*** techniques (secular version of ***God's Storehouse Principle***), and for her "***Networking Strategies"*** topic, especially her "***Networking Through Six Degrees of Separation"*** approach (included within ***God's Storehouse Principle***), *which improves the success ratio for every conference attendee, especially first time attendees while meeting people within other businesses and industries within the working sessions and the conference EXPO. In addition, she is often asked to provide 'break-out' seminars throughout the scheduled conference days and the number of the attendee always exceeds the capacity of the room with people squeezing in, leaning against the wall and the water table in the back of the room.*

Her conference talks are known for being results oriented, action packed and exciting, while each person is impacted with a different insight, giving them the ability to develop a new awareness and understanding of their capabilities in life. She receives feedback from many of the participants that after attending one of her conference talks, they have finally realized how to practically reach their full potential. Because of her unique approach and her understanding of business strategies and industry trends, she has been interviewed on local, regional, national and international radio and TV programs.

Books by Author

GOD'S STOREHOUSE
PRINCIPLE

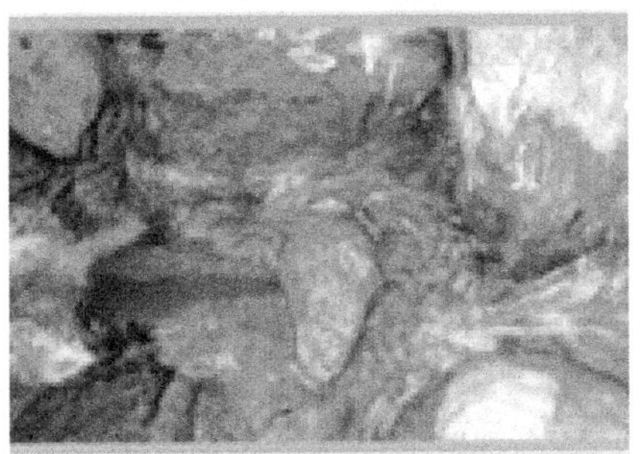

GOD'S STOREHOUSE PRINCIPLE WORKBOOK

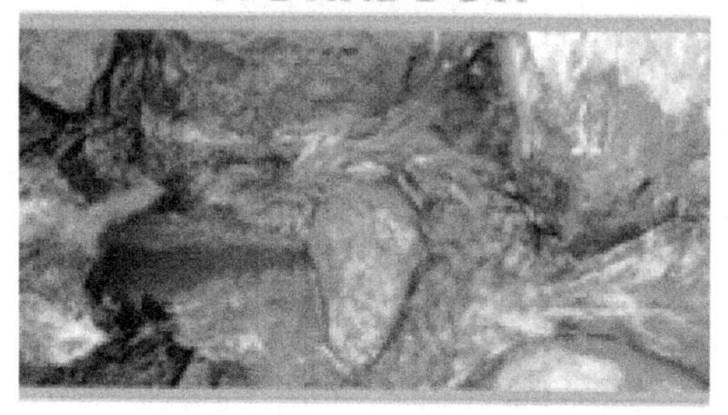

Individually and Globally
We Are The Church, The Body of Christ
Responsible For Restoring The
Flow of God's Blessings

SHEILA HOLM

Nation Restoration

Restoring finances, laws and life after Identity Theft, a crime that has become an industry unto itself.

Sheila Holm

A WAKE UP CALL: IT'S RESTORATION TIME!

MYSTERIES REVEALED: HOW AND WHEN THE CHURCH WAS DECEIVED AND WHAT IS REQUIRED FOR FULL RESTORATION.

SHEILA HOLM

IN SEARCH OF WIGGLESWORTH

A JOURNEY WHICH SPEAKS TO THE VERY CORE OF WHAT IT MEANS TO BE A TRUE BROTHER AND SISTER IN CHRIST!

SHEILA HOLM

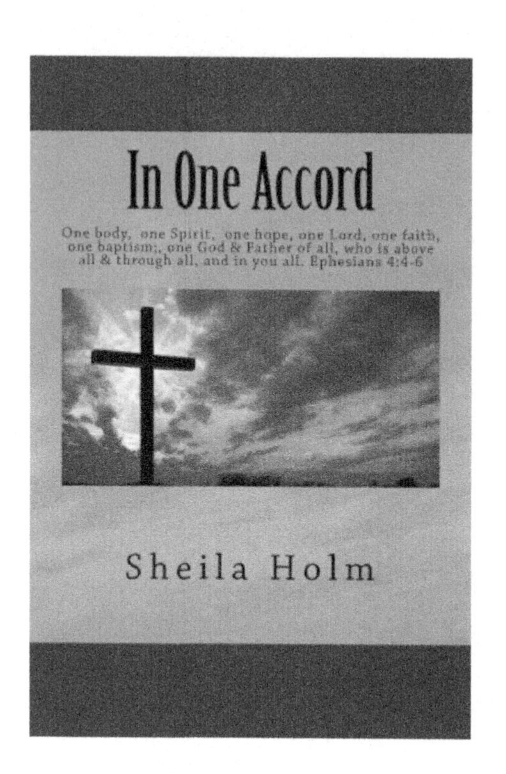

A PECULIAR PEOPLE

DISCIPLESHIP OF PECULIAR PEOPLE BY PECULIAR PEOPLE

SHEILA HOLM

ALWAYS
SPEAK LIFE

FOR THE EYES OF THE LORD ARE ON THE RIGHTEOUS, AND HIS EARS ARE OPEN TO THEIR PRAYERS ... 1 PETER 3:12

SHEILA HOLM

CHRISTMAS

MYSTERIES UNCOVERED & REVEALED: TRUTH REGARDING THE BIRTH OF THE MESSIAH, HIDDEN SINCE 300 AD

SHEILA HOLM

FOREWORD BY
KEN BLANCHARD
Seven
Step
Business
Plan
SHEILA
HOLM
"Seven Step Business Plan is the first and only book to provide a simple format for every business to be able to prepare and update their business plan."
—Ken Blanchard,
The One Minute Manager

About the Author

God showed the exact plan of ***God's Currency*** to Sheila with His orchestration of all arrangements while God took Sheila's hand and traveled with her while equipping and training her.

God has taken Sheila around the globe, going church to church, business to business, nation to nation. He fulfills upon His promises within His scriptures. He has equipped and trained her, while He:

- Sends her forth without an extra coin or tunic.
- Arranges flights and accommodations in each nation.
- Introduces her before she arrives.
- Lifts her up and encourages her.
- Seats her before governors and kings.
- Fills her as an empty vessel.
- Shares His wisdom and word of knowledge.
- Blesses and heals the people in her path.

- Comforts her and re-encourages her.
- Touches people individually in conferences/multitude.
- Speaks through her with power and authority.
- Addresses situations the body of Christ is facing.
- Speaks through her so the people hear His words in their own language.
- Directs her path to speak life into each situation whether God sends people to her to be re-encouraged or he asks her to pray with a pastor, the church, or someone in a store or a restaurant, etc.

Many confirm she walks in the five-fold ministry. She does not use a title because God does the work while He sends her as an apostle and prophet and He orchestrates all arrangements for her to preach, teach, and evangelize.

People attending the conferences often say her segments are like watching someone walk out of the bible, share for a while and then, go right back in the bible, aka continue upon her journey in HIStory.

Ministry email: hisbest4usorders@gmail.com

Use the subject line: ***God's Currency***

Web site: http://hisbest4us.org

Facebook: HISBest4us

Dare To Believe, Then Command

Smith Wigglesworth – 1919

"Verily, verily, I say unto you; He that believeth on Me, the works that I do shall he do also: and greater works than these shall he do; because I go unto My Father. And whatsoever ye shall ask in My name, that will I do, that the Father may be glorified in the Son. If ye shall ask any thing in My name, I will do it." John 14:12-14.

Jesus is speaking here, and the Spirit of God can take these words of His and make them real to us. "He that believeth on Me... greater works than these shall he do." What a word! Is it true? If you want the truth, where will you get it? "Thy word is truth," Christ said to the Father. When you take up God's Word you get the truth. God is not the author of confusion or error, but He sends forth His light and truth to lead us into His holy habitation, where we receive a revelation of the truth like unto the noon day in all its clearness.

The Word of God works effectually in us as we believe it. It changes us and brings us into new fellowship with the Father, with the Son, and with the Holy Spirit, into a holy communion, into an unwavering faith, into a mighty assurance, and it will make us partakers of the very nature and likeness of God as we receive His great and exceeding precious promises and believe them. Faith cometh by hearing, and hearing by the Word of God. Faith is the operative power.

We read that Christ opened the understanding of His disciples, and He will open up our understanding and our hearts and will show us wonderful things that we should never know but for the mighty revelation and enlightenment of the Spirit that He gives to us.

I do not know of any greater words than those found in Romans 4:16, "Therefore it is of faith, that it might be by grace." Grace is God's benediction coming right down to you, and when you open the door to Him—that is an act of faith—He does all you want and will fulfill all your desires. "It is of faith, that it might be by grace." You open the way for God to work as you believe His Word, and God will come in and supply your every need all along the way.

Our Lord Jesus said to His disciples and He says to us in this passage in the 14th of John, "You have seen Me work and you know how I work. You shall do the very same things that I am doing, and greater things shall you do, because I am going to the Father, and as you make petition in My name I will work. I will do what you ask, and by this the Father shall be glorified."

Did any one ever work as He did? I do not mean His carpentering. I refer to His work in the hearts of the people. He drew them to Him. They came with their needs, with their sicknesses, with their oppression, and He relieved them all. This royal Visitor, who came from the Father to express His love, talked to men, spent time with them in their homes, found out their every need. He went about doing good and healing all who were oppressed of the devil, and He said to them and He says to us, "You see what I have been doing, healing the sick, relieving the oppressed, casting out demons. The works that I do shall ye do also." Dare you believe? Will you take up the work that He left and carry it on?

"He that believeth on Me!" What is this? What does it mean? How can just believing bring these things to pass? What virtue is there in it? There is virtue in these words because He declares them. If we will receive this word and declare it, the greater works shall be accomplished. This is a positive declaration of His, "He that believeth on Me, greater works than these shall he do," but unbelief has hindered our progress in the realm of the spiritual.

Put away unbelief. Open your heart to God's grace. Then God will come in and place in you a definite faith. He wants to remove every obstruction that is in the world before you. By His grace He will enable you to be so established in His truth, so strong in the Lord and in the power of His might, that whatever comes across your path to obstruct you, you can arise in divine power and rebuke and destroy it.

It is a matter of definite and clear understanding between us and God. To recognize that Christ has a life force to put into us, changes everything that we dare to *believe* it will change. He that believes that Jesus is the Christ overcomes the world. Because we believe that Jesus is the Christ, the essence of divine life is in us by faith and causes a perfect separation between us and the world. We have no room for sin. It is a joyful thing for us to be doing that which is right. He will cause that abundance of grace to so flow into our hearts that sin shall not have dominion over us. Sin shall not have dominion; nor sickness, nor affliction. "He that believeth"—he that dares to believe—he that dares to trust—will see victory over every oppression of the enemy.

A needy creature came to me in a meeting, all withered and wasted. He had no hope. There was absolute death in his eyes. He was so helpless he had to have some one on each side to bear him up. He came to me and said in a whisper, "Can you help me?" Will Jesus answer? "He that believeth on Me, the works that I do shall he do also; and greater works than these.... Behold, I give you power... over all the power of the enemy." These are the words of our Lord Jesus. It is not our word but the word of the Lord, and as this word is in us He can make it like a burning passion in us. We make the Word of God as we believe it our own. We receive the Word and we have the very life of Christ in us. We become supernatural by the power of God. We find this power working through every part of our being.

Now Christ gives us something besides faith. He gives us something to make faith effectual. Whatsoever you desire, if you believe in your heart you shall have. Christ said, “Have faith in God. For verily I say unto you, That whosoever shall say unto this mountain, Be thou removed, and be thou cast into the sea; and shall not doubt in his heart, but shall believe that those things which he saith shall come to pass; he shall have whatsoever he saith. Therefore I say unto you, What things soever ye desire, when ye pray, believe that ye receive them, and ye shall have them.” Mark 11:22-24. Whatsoever he saith! Dare to say in faith and it shall be done. These things have been promised by Christ and He does not lie.

This afflicted man stood before me helpless and withered. He had had cancer in his stomach. The physicians had operated upon him to take away the cancer from the stomach, but complications had arisen with the result that no food could enter the man’s stomach. He could not swallow anything. So in order to keep him alive they made a hole in his stomach and put in a tube about nine inches long with a cup at the top, and he was fed with liquid through this tube. For three months he had been just kept alive but was like a skeleton.

What was I to say to him? “If thou wouldest believe, thou shouldest see the glory of God.”

Here was the word of Christ, “He that believeth on me, the works that I do shall he do also, and greater works than these shall he do; because I go unto My Father.” The Word of God is truth. Christ is with the Father and grants us our requests, and makes these things manifest, if we believe. What should I do in the presence of a case like this? “Believe the Word.” So I believed the Word which says, “He shall have whatsoever he saith.” Mark 11:23. I said, “Go home, and have a good supper.” He said, “I cannot swallow.”

“Go home, and have a good supper,” I repeated. “On the authority of the Word of God I say it. Christ says that he that believes that these things which he says shall come to pass he shall have whatsoever he says. So I say, Go home in the name of Jesus, and have a good supper.”

He went home. Supper was prepared. Many times he had had food in his mouth but had always been forced to spit it out again. But I dared to believe that he would be able to swallow that night. So that man filled his mouth full as he had done before, and because some one dared to believe God’s Word and said to him, “You shall have a good supper in the name of Jesus,” when he chewed his food it went down in the normal way into his stomach, and he ate until he was quite satisfied.

He and his family went to bed filled with joy. The next morning when they arose they were filled with the same joy.

Life had begun again. Naturally he looked down to see the hole that had been made in his stomach by the physicians. But God knew that he did not want two holes, and so when God opened the normal passage He closed the other hole in his stomach. This is the kind of God we have all the time, a God who knows, a God who acts, and brings things to pass when we believe. Dare to believe, and then dare to speak and you shall have whatsoever you say if you doubt not.

A woman came to me one night and inquired, “Can I hear again? Is it possible for me to hear again? I have had several operations and the drums of my ears have been taken away.” I said, “If God has not forgotten how to make drums for ears you can hear again.” Do you think God has forgotten? What does God forget? He forgets our sins, when we are forgiven, but He has not forgotten how to make drums for ears.

Not long ago the power of God was very much upon a meeting that I was holding. I was telling the people that they could be healed without my going to them. If they would rise up I would pray and the Lord would heal. There was a man who put up his hand. I said, “Cannot that man rise?” The folks near him said he could not, and lifted him hp. The Lord healed him the ribs that were broken were knit together again and were healed.

There was such faith in the place that a little girl cried out, "Please, gentleman, come to me." You could not see her, she was so small. The mother said, "My little girl wants you to come." So I went down there to this child, who although fourteen years of age was very small. She said with tears streaming down her face, "Will you pray for me?" I said, "Dare you believe?" She said, "O yes." I prayed and placed my hands on her head in the name of Jesus.

"Mother," she said, "I am being healed. Take these things off—take them all off." The mother loosed straps and bands and then the child said, "Mother, I am sure I am healed. Take these off." She had straps on her legs and an iron on her foot about 3½ inches deep. She asked her mother to unstrap her. Her mother took off the straps. There were not many people with dry eyes as they saw that girl walk about with legs just as normal as when she was born. God healed her right away. What did it? She had cried, "Please, gentleman, come to me," and her longing was coupled with faith. May the Lord help us to be just like a simple child.

God has hidden these things from the wise and prudent, but He reveals them to babes. There is something in childlike faith in God that makes us dare to believe, and then to act. Whatever there is in your life that is bound, the name of Jesus and the power of that name will break it if you will only believe. Christ says, "If ye shall ask any thing in My name, I will do it." God will be glorified in Christ when you receive the overflowing life that comes from Christ in response to your faith.

Dare to believe. Do you think that truth is put into the Word to mock you? Don't you see that God really means that you should live in the world to relieve the oppression of the world? God answers us that we shall be quickened, be molded afresh, that the Word of God shall change everything that needs to be changed, both in us and in others, as we dare to believe and as we command things to be done. "Whosoever shall say unto this mountain, Be thou removed, and be thou cast into the sea; and shall not doubt in his heart, but shall believe that those things which he saith shall come to pass, he shall have whatsoever he saith."

Published in the Pentecostal Evangel on March 30, 1940

America was Founded upon Faith as the Path to Freedom and Liberty

Faith Monument

On the main pedestal stands the heroic figure of "Faith" with her right hand pointing toward heaven and her left hand clutching the Bible. Upon the four buttresses also are seated figures emblematical of the principles upon which the Pilgrims founded their Commonwealth, each having a symbol referring to the Bible that "Faith" possesses; counter-clockwise from the feet of "Faith" are Morality, Law, Education, and Liberty. Each was carved from a solid block of granite, posed in the sitting position upon chairs with a high relief on either side of minor characteristics. Under "Morality" stand "Prophet" and "Evangelist"; under "Law" stand "Justice" and "Mercy"; under "Education" are "Youth" and "Wisdom"; and under "Liberty" stand "Tyranny Overthrown" and "Peace". On the face of the buttresses, beneath these figures are high reliefs in marble, representing scenes from Pilgrim history. Under "Morality" is "Embarcation"; under "Law" is "Treaty"; under "Education" is "Compact"; and under "Freedom" is "Landing". Upon the four faces of the main pedestal are large panels for records. The front panel is inscribed as follows:

"National Monument to the Forefathers: Erected by a grateful people in remembrance of their labors, sacrifices and sufferings for the cause of civil and religious liberty." The right and left panels contain the names of those who came over in the *Mayflower.*

The rear panel, which was not engraved until recently, contains a quote from Governor William Bradford's famous history, ***Of Plymouth Plantation***:

> ***"Thus out of small beginnings greater things have been produced by His hand that made all things of nothing and gives being to all things that are; and as one small candle may light a thousand, so the light here kindled hath shone unto many, yea in some sort to our whole nation; let the glorious name of Jehovah have all praise."***

Made in the USA
Monee, IL
04 May 2022